The
Ben Franklin Book
of Easy and Incredible Experiments

A Franklin Institute Science Museum Book

Illustrations by Cheryl Kirk Noll

JOHN WILEY & SONS, INC.

New York • Chichester • Brisbane • Toronto • Singapore

Edited by Lisa Jo Rudy

This text is printed on acid-free paper.

Copyright © 1995 by Franklin Institute Science Museum
Published by John Wiley & Sons, Inc.

Illustrations © 1995 by Cheryl Kirk Noll

The publisher and the author have made every reasonable effort to ensure that the experiments and activities in this book are safe when conducted as instructed but assume no responsibility for any damage caused or sustained while performing the experiments or activities in this book. Parents, guardians, and/or teachers should supervise young readers who undertake the experiments and activities in this book.

Library of Congress Cataloging-in-Publication Data

The Ben Franklin book of easy and incredible experiments / Franklin Institute
   Science Museum
         p.   cm.
      Includes index.
      ISBN 0-471-07639-2—ISBN 0-471-07638-4 (paper)
      1. Science—Experiments.   2. Science—Experiments—Juvenile literature.
   3. Engineering—Experiments.   4. Engineering—Experiments—Juvenile literature.
   5. Franklin, Benjamin. 1706-1790.   [1. Science—Experiments.   2. Engineering—
   Experiments.   3. Experiments.]   I. Franklin Institute (Philadelphia, Pa.).
   Science Museum.
   Q182.3B46   1995
   507.8—dc20   94-45549

Printed in the United States of America

10   9   8   7   6   5   4   3   2

Preface

At the Franklin Institute we believe learning about science should be fun and that people learn best by trying things out for themselves. That's why our museum is filled with hundreds of what we call hands-on devices, or exhibits that are made for people to explore and experiment with.

As you'll find out when you use this book, Ben Franklin believed in learning by doing. He used the scientific method as his guide, observing, experimenting, and hypothesizing. His experimentation led to many important inventions—the lightning rod, the Franklin stove, bifocals, and even a musical instrument called the armonica.

The activities in this book are organized around six subjects that especially interested Ben: observation and experimentation, meteorology, electricity, sound and music, paper and printing, and lenses and vision. We encourage you to use the activities in this book as a starting point for further exploration and discovery. Like Ben Franklin, your work could one day lead to the creation of many great things.

Happy experimenting!

Dennis Wint
President
The Franklin Institute

Acknowledgments

Material for this book was provided by the Franklin Institute staff, who searched their files for science activities that reflected topic areas relevant to Benjamin Franklin. The Institute wishes to thank Lisa Rudy for taking the hundreds of activities that were sourced, winnowing them down, organizing them, doing additional research, and writing the manuscript.

Contents

Introduction

Benjamin Franklin of Philadelphia, Pennsylvania, was the first great American scientist. His famous electricity experiments were an important part of the development of our modern world. In his lifetime, Franklin was honored by the great scientific societies of Europe. Today, he is known as one of the most significant scientists in history.

Benjamin Franklin: Scientist, Inventor, Patriot

When Benjamin Franklin was born in 1706, the eighteenth century had barely begun. People were beginning to change the way they thought about the world. For the first time, people tried to understand the laws that govern the physical universe and the natural world, and to use that knowledge to help people improve their lives. We call the eighteenth century the Age of Enlightenment. These new ideas marked the beginning of modern science.

In the United States at that time, only a few Americans were familiar with science. But even as a young man, Ben was always open to new ideas. He read new books, met scientists from Europe, and asked many questions. His curiosity about the world around him was boundless. He would first ask, "How does it work?" Then he would try to solve the problem step by step by breaking it down into smaller questions and examining each one carefully. This process of experimentation, called the **scientific method,** seems like common sense to us now. But 200 years ago, it was not a common way of thinking.

Ben Franklin was a serious scientist and a practical man. He looked for a useful way to use the new knowledge from each experiment. For instance, he used his observations of the Gulf Stream to speed the delivery of mail; he created a safety device called a lightning rod after experimenting with electricity, and he invented bifocal eyeglasses after finding that he needed two pairs of glasses—one to see things at a distance and another to read up close. You will learn about each experiment in this book.

He was also a man with a strong sense of humor. For example, when he could not think of a useful purpose for electricity, he proposed a picnic on the banks of the Schuylkill River in Philadelphia where the dinner turkey "would be killed by electrical shock."

Franklin advised his son, "Be always employed in something useful." Following his own advice, Franklin established the first fire insurance company in America, is thought to be the father of the United States Weather Bureau, was the first to propose daylight savings time, organized the postal system, and was our first Postmaster General.

Franklin helped Thomas Jefferson write the Declaration of Independence, founded the University of Pennsylvania, established the first successful circulating library, and invented a musical instrument, called the glass armonica. He was also the only person to sign all four of the great state papers that achieved independence for the United States—the Declaration of Independence, the Treaty of Alliance with France, the Treaty of Peace with England, and the Constitution of the United States.

Few people in history have accomplished as much as Benjamin Franklin. His contributions range from the areas of government and business to those of medicine, science, and even music. If Ben could visit our modern world, he would discover that many of his best ideas have been improved upon—but are still recognizably his. Part of Ben's plan was that he should be remembered in the future, and he most certainly is!

The Franklin Institute Science Museum

We remember Benjamin Franklin in many ways. The Franklin Institute Science Museum in Philadelphia is dedicated to the spirit of Ben Franklin. Founded in 1934, it now serves one million visitors a year. True to Franklin's spirit, the museum offers hundreds of opportunities to experiment with exhibits. People can walk through a giant model of a human heart, climb aboard a 350-ton Baldwin locomotive, and experiment with examples of technology that are shaping our future. The Franklin Institute includes a four-story, wraparound Omnimax movie theater, a planetarium, an outdoor observatory, a working weather station, and the Benjamin Franklin National Memorial.

About This Book

We hope this book helps you search for new ways to see things. Each chapter focuses on a subject Franklin worked on and cared about. Each one contains experiments and activities that will help you think creatively and do things like make a weather station, create an orchestra, or build an optical toy shop.

At the end of each chapter is a list of resources and ideas. This is where the fun really begins, because you can use your own creativity to discover new ways to do things. Like Ben Franklin, you can use your imagination to explore the world, discover how things work, and find new ways to solve old problems.

Good luck, and enjoy!

The Life of Benjamin Franklin
1706–1790

1706 Born January 17 in Boston, Massachusetts, the youngest son of Josiah and Abiah Franklin.

1718 Apprenticed to his brother James, a Boston printer.

1723 Ran away to Philadelphia, where he found work at Samuel Keimer's printing house.

1728–1731 Formed the first printing partnership. Married Deborah Read in 1730, and became sole owner of the printing business. Published first edition of the *Pennsylvania Gazette*. Founded the first circulating library in North America.

1732 Published the first edition of *Poor Richard's Almanack*.

1733–1745 Was appointed to his first public office, clerk of the General Assembly of Pennsylvania. Invented the Franklin stove. In 1737, was appointed Deputy Postmaster of Philadelphia. By 1743, owned and ran three printing houses in three different colonies.

1746 Began first experiments in electricity.

1747–1748 Retired from active business to continue electrical experiments and pursue a public service career that lasted 40 years.

1749 Helped found the Pennsylvania Academy, which later became the University of Pennsylvania.

1750–1751 Elected to the Pennsylvania Assembly, where he served for 14 years. Helped found the Pennsylvania Hospital, America's first charity hospital.

1752-1754 Established the first fire insurance company in North America. Conducted famous kite experiment. Erected lightning rods in Philadelphia. Received the Copley Medal of the Royal Society of London for research in electricity. Was appointed Deputy Postmaster General of North America. Wrote a plan for a union of the colonies for security and defense.

1762 Returned to Philadelphia and mapped postal routes in the colonies. Invented the glass armonica.

1764-1765 Traveled to England to represent the colony of Pennsylvania; charted the Gulf Stream.

1771-1772 Began writing his famous *Autobiography*. Presented the petition of the first Continental Congress to the King of England.

1775 Returned to Philadelphia. Was elected to the Second Continental Congress. Proposed the Articles of Confederation. Was unanimously elected Postmaster General of the American colonies by Congress.

1776-1778 Was appointed to the committee to draft the Declaration of Independence. Went to France to obtain financing for the American troops. Negotiated treaties with France.

1779-1781 Was appointed by Congress to negotiate peace with Great Britain.

1783-1784 Signed a peace treaty with Great Britain. Invented bifocal eyeglasses.

1785-1786 Was elected President of Pennsylvania. Invented an instrument for taking books down from high shelves, called the long arm.

1789 Wrote his last public letter, urging the abolition of slavery.

1790 Wrote his last letter to Thomas Jefferson. Died April 17 in his home in Philadelphia at the age of 84.

Chapter 1

Using Your Head

Ben Franklin was famous for his curiosity. Even when he sat in long, dull meetings or traveled from place to place, he always found something to interest him. When he could, he conducted scientific **experiments** to keep himself occupied. During his ocean voyages from America to Europe and back, for example, he studied the temperature and depth of the water; the weather patterns around him; and even the way objects (such as wooden boxes) responded to the sea air.

Ben asked questions about things other people did not even think about. Why does snow melt faster on dark surfaces than on light surfaces? What is lightning? How do storms travel? What causes ocean water to be warmer in some places and cooler in others? More important than just asking these questions, Ben Franklin went out and answered them by observing and experimenting. Then, he went one step further: he used his discoveries to invent and build real, useful tools to make life easier. For example, his observations and discoveries about hot and cold led him to invent the efficient Franklin stove. And his experiments with electricity allowed him to invent the lightning rod. We still use both the Franklin stove and the lightning rod today.

DO IT: A Hot-and-Cold Experiment

Ben Franklin corresponded with Polly Stevenson, the daughter of his landlady in London, for a long time. In one letter, he described an experiment he conducted to find out whether dark colors become hot faster than light colors. Here is part of one letter to Polly:

I took a number of little square pieces of cloth . . . of various colors. There were black, deep blue, lighter blue, green, purple, red, yellow, white and other colors or shades of colors. I laid them all out upon the snow on a bright sunshiny morning.

You can easily repeat Franklin's experiment. Perhaps you will draw the same conclusions he did.

Materials

a snowy yard, or a baking pan containing shaved ice
squares of cloth cut from the same kind of fabric (cotton, linen, and so on). Each square should be a different color, with the colors ranging from very dark to very light.
a sunny day, or a bright lamp (such as a sunlamp)

Procedure

1. Make sure the snow or shaved ice has a flat surface.

2. Place the squares of cloth on the snow or ice. If you are using a baking pan, place it outside in a sunny spot (or directly under the lamp).

3. Let the squares sit for a half hour; then, check them. What happened to the snow or ice under each square? If you don't observe any changes, let the squares sit for another half hour. Keep checking the squares until you observe a change. What happened?

This is what Ben Franklin told Polly Stevenson about the change he saw:

> In a few hours . . . the black, being warmed most by the sun, was sunk so low as to be below the stroke of the sun's rays; the dark blue almost as low, the lighter blue not quite as much as the dark, the other colors less as they were lighter; and the quite white remained on the surface of the snow, not having entered it at all.

Did you obtain the same results Franklin did? If not, what do you think caused the difference?

Franklin, as he often did, took his discovery a step further. Perhaps, he reasoned, there was a use for his finding that dark fabrics absorb heat more rapidly than light fabrics. What possibilities can you imagine?

Here is what Franklin wrote Polly about his ideas:

> May we not learn . . . that black clothes are not so fit to wear in a hot sunny climate or season as white ones. . . . That soldiers and seamen, who must march and labor in the sun, should in [hot places] have a uniform of white, that summer hats, for men or women, should be white, as repelling that heat which gives headaches to many. . . .

Are your ideas similar to Franklin's? Where do you agree or disagree? What effect might Franklin's ideas have had on summer fashions?

Learning to Observe

Observation is more than just seeing, hearing, smelling, tasting, and feeling. It is paying attention to what goes on around you. It means noticing objects, people, and—especially—patterns. For example, you may have noticed that there is a tree in your yard. But have you noticed the patterns of the leaves? The textures of the leaves and bark? Do you know at what time of year the leaves begin to bud? The kinds of seeds the tree drops, and when the seeds fall? The color the leaves turn in the fall? Whether the leaves start to turn color before or after the first frost?

When you closely observe patterns in nature, you learn a great deal about the natural world. When you observe patterns in human behavior, you learn a lot about people. Ben Franklin studied patterns in the natural world and in human behavior, and his observations gave him extraordinary insights. But observation isn't always as easy as it sounds. The games in this section will help you sharpen your observation abilities—and may show you how tricky it can be to become a good observer.

DO IT: An Observation Game

You can play this fun, simple game with another person (or a group of people) to sharpen your observation skills.

Materials

timer
at least 2 people

Procedure

1. Select one person to be observed, and one person to be the observer.

2. Ask the observer to study the person to be observed about 2 minutes. The observer should try to notice everything about the person—from a part in the hair to a knot in a shoe.

3. Ask the observer to leave the room. While he or she is gone, the person who is being observed must change three items of personal appearance. Some possibilities are unbuttoning a button, rolling up a sleeve, untying a shoe.

4. When the observer returns, he or she must figure out what changes the person being observed made. Can the observer name all three changes? Did the observer guess things that had not been changed?

What makes this game easy or difficult? What could make it easier or more difficult?

Observing is sometimes hard, because people ordinarily ignore most of the information their senses give them. If we constantly noticed every sound, sight, feeling, and smell, we would not be able to concentrate on anything. To discover how much there is to observe every minute of every day, try this experiment:

DO IT: Paying Attention to It All!

Material
watch or timer
pencil
paper

Procedure

1. Check your watch or set your timer for 5 minutes.

2. Sit down and make a list of everything you can observe from your chair. Check all your senses: What do you smell? What do you feel? Don't forget to notice the pressure of your chair against your skin, the texture of the pencil against your fingers, and so forth.

3. After 5 minutes, put down your pencil. Have you listed everything you noticed? How many items are on your list?

4. After you have checked your list, pay attention to your senses again. Did you stop feeling the chair and the pencil while you were reading your list?

━━━━━━━━

Human brains automatically "tune out" sensory information that doesn't seem important. That's why you may temporarily forget that you're hungry or tired when something exciting or frightening is occurring in your life. It's also why you might not notice changes in the weather until the rain begins, or why you might not hear your mother calling you when you're busy playing.

If it is hard to keep track of what your senses tell you, keeping patterns in your mind is even more difficult. For example, it may take you weeks to notice that your father always wears his blue tie on Wednesdays. You may have noticed the tie, and you may have observed that your dad wears it fairly often. But for you to recognize the pattern of "every Wednesday" requires that you pay special attention to details. This observation activity will help you discover how difficult it can be to pick out patterns:

DO IT: Black Magic

Materials

4 or more people

Procedure

1. Explain to the group that they will be playing a game called Black Magic.

2. Select one person from the group. Take him or her aside and say, "I am going to send you out of the room. While you are gone, we will choose one object in the room. Then, when you return, I will touch a series of objects and ask you if this is the one the group chose. You will know which object the group chose because it will be the first object I touch after I have touched something that is black."

3. Send the person out of the room. With the rest of the group, choose any object in the room (a fan, a window, and so on).

4. Call the person back into the room. First, touch one object at a time, each time asking, "Is this the one?" The person should respond, "no" to every object. Then, touch a black object, and ask, "Is this the one?" The person would respond, "no," but respond "yes" when you touch the next object.

5. Ask the rest of the group if they can figure out how the person knew which object they had chosen. Remind them that the name of the game is *black* magic. They may not see the pattern the first time—or even the second time. You may have to perform your black magic three or four more times before the people catch on to the pattern.

Unless your group of friends already knew the game, it might have been hard for them to see the pattern—the object touched after a black object is the one that was picked. Why do you think it is difficult to see a pattern like that one? What kinds of patterns are easy to see, and what kinds are difficult to see? Why?

If you like, think up some other kinds of games that will sharpen your observation skills. Then, when you're ready, do the activities in the next sections of this chapter.

Observation and Innovation

Ben Franklin was a top-notch observer. He saw patterns in the natural world and in human nature where no one else did. For example, he noticed that heat from logs in fireplaces disappears up the chimney. Most people didn't really notice that heat escapes this way. Instead, they just kept throwing logs on the fire when they got cold—which, in the winter, was most of the time! The more logs they piled on the fire, the more irritated their eyes became with smoke and soot, and the dirtier the house became.

Ben decided he wanted to develop a stove that would keep the warm air in the house. His search began with a series of experiments based on using air and fire. Through these experiments, Franklin learned that air expands as it gets warmer, taking up more space and weighing less than the air around it. He also discovered that air **contracts,** or shrinks, when it cools, so that it occupies less space and weighs more than the air around it.

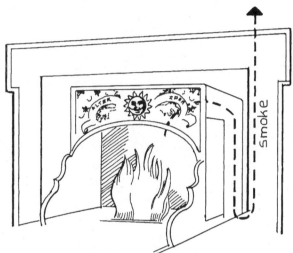

Franklin also observed stoves in Europe that reheated stale air, keeping the house warm, but very stuffy. So, based on what he had noticed and what he already knew, Franklin redesigned the European stove—so that it burned less fuel and at the same time, created more warmth, all without making the house stuffy.

Franklin didn't invent the stove. But he designed a better stove, based on his observations of fireplaces and stoves that already existed. This kind of creative work is called **innovation.**

DO IT: An Innovative Idea
An **innovator** takes something that already exists and thinks of a new or better way to use it. This activity will give you practice innovating. The process of coming up with new ideas—no matter how silly or how impractical—is called **brainstorming.**

Materials
pile of rubber bands
pencil
sheet of paper
friends or family members

Procedure
1. Sit around a table with your friends or family. Place the pile of rubber bands in front of you and a pencil and sheet of paper next to you.

2. Observe the rubber bands. What are the qualities of rubber bands? Make a list of them. Your observations may include the color, shape, texture, and smell of the rubber bands.

3. What can rubber bands do? As a group, try to come up with ten innovative ways to use rubber bands. Be creative! To get started, you might want to mention a few ordinary uses: "Rubber bands can be used to hold hair in a ponytail, or hold a stack of papers together. They can also be used for _____."

4. As individuals suggest ideas—no matter how silly—write them down. Can you come up with ten ideas? With more than ten?

5. Try putting a few of your ideas into practice. Do they work? Which of your ideas are most useful? Did you learn anything you didn't know about rubber bands?

Observation and Invention

Ben Franklin was one of the most famous **inventors** in history. Inventors, unlike innovators, build something brand new—something that has never existed before. One of Ben's most useful (and simplest) **inventions** was the long arm. Like most people, Franklin often had to reach things, like books, that were on tall shelves, and beyond the reach of his arms. As we all do, he climbed up on chairs or ladders to get to those things. Then, he realized there was a better way.

To reach books that were on the top shelf, Ben invented a gadget he called the long arm. The long arm was a long pole with a gripper on one end and a cord to close the gripper If you look around in grocery stores and bookstores, you will probably see gadgets very much like Ben's long arm still in use.

Most inventions and innovations are designed to solve a specific problem or serve a particular need. Inventors and innovators discover these problems or needs through observation. Then, they analyze the problems, consider possible solutions, and experiment with the possible solutions until they arrive at a solution that works. Innovators may find that they can improve upon someone else's invention (like Ben's stove). Inventors may find that they need to come up with a brand-new way to solve a problem (like Ben's long arm).

long arm

DO IT: Innovation and Invention, Part One

Inventors and innovators solve problems in new and creative ways. First, however, they observe the world around them and ask questions.

Materials

all of your senses
one object, or an area that includes a group of objects
timer
pencil
2 sheets of paper
friend (optional)

Procedure

By yourself or with a friend, observe all you can about an object or an area that includes a group of objects (such as a rosebush or a playground, a cat or a parking lot) for a full 5 minutes. Make a list of everything you observe. If you can (and it is safe), use all five of your senses to increase your range of observations. When 5 minutes are up, read your list. If you are with a friend, compare your lists.

How many of the objects on your lists did you notice for the first time? How many of the objects you observed raised questions in your mind? For instance, if you spent your time looking at a rosebush, you may have noticed that some of the blossoms were drooping. Did you wonder why? Put a checkmark next to the observations that raised questions for you. Then, write down the questions on a separate sheet of paper. Save the list for the next activity.

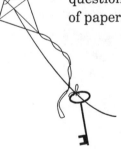

DO IT: Innovation and Invention, Part Two

After Franklin made observations, he often conducted experiments to find out why certain of the things he noticed happened. Sometimes his experiments were simple activities he could do in his backyard—such as the experiment with the cloth and the snow (p. 8).

But sometimes Franklin's experiments required research and hard work. For example, when Ben was Postmaster General of the American colonies, he observed that the mail sent by ship from America to England arrived in good time. But the mail sent by ship from England to America took two weeks longer to arrive. This happened over and over again. The pattern made Ben wonder why.

He had some ideas: maybe the English sailors were lazy; maybe the American ships were better built. But he needed an answer.

Ben Franklin asked his question of a Nantucket sea captain, Timothy Folger. Folger explained to Ben that a strong current in the Atlantic Ocean helped to speed American ships eastward toward England. But on the return trip west, the current slowed ships down.

Ben worked with Folger to determine just where the current ran. He watched the progress of ships to see whether his calculations were correct. Finally, he drew maps of the ocean that showed the location of the current.

All of this information helped Ben speed up the mail delivery. He told the captains of his mail ships to take advantage of the rapid current on the way to England and to avoid the current when returning to America.

Ben named the current the Gulf Stream, because it originated in the Gulf of Mexico. His observations have been important to shipping navigation and weather observation for over 200 years.

Ben had a specific question to answer: Why does mail from England to America arrive two weeks late? Instead of shrugging his shoulders, he looked for an answer. He had some ideas—but he did not assume his ideas were correct. Instead, Ben worked hard to uncover the possibilities, tested his **calculations** (results of using mathematical processes), and charted his final answers.

Materials

the list of questions from the activity "Innovation and Invention, Part One"
pencil
sheet of paper

Procedure

1. Return to your list of questions. Pick one that interests you. Then, think about what the answer to the question might be. Write down all the possible answers you can imagine. For instance, if your question is, Why are the rose blossoms drooping? You might write down several possible answers: because the rosebush doesn't get enough water; because the bush is getting too much sun; because the dog has dug up the soil around the bush.

   All of these answers may be correct, or only one may be correct, or there may be another answer that you haven't thought of yet. You can eliminate some possible answers right away. For example, you can check whether the soil around the rosebush has been dug up. If it hasn't, you can eliminate the dog as the culprit. But how can you find out what the problem really is? The answer is, you experiment.

2. Pick one possible answer to your question. An educated guess about the outcome of an experiment is called a **hypothesis.** In the case of the rosebush, you might guess: The bush is not getting enough water.

3. Test that one possible answer to your question. By testing only one possible answer at a time, you can determine which answer is correct. In the case of the rosebush, you might try giving the bush plenty of water for a week.

4. Analyze your results. In this example, you would pay attention to how the rosebush responds to the extra water. If it does not perk up, it's time to pick another possible answer and test that one. If the bush stops drooping, it *may* be because of the water, but it *could* be caused by something else.

When you test a hypothesis through experimentation, you end up making conclusions—such as the conclusion that lack of water probably made the rose blossoms droop. But it's not always quite this simple! Sometimes more than one factor may be at work. For example, the rosebush may also have been getting more sun while you were giving it more water. You know now that this system of experimentation is called the scientific method.

Ben Franklin was a doer. He always had ideas about how to use his discoveries, and many of his most useful inventions and innovations came out of his own experiments. Based on his cloth and snow experiment, Ben found it was a good idea to wear light-colored clothes in summer. Through his discoveries and experiments with the Gulf Stream, Ben was able to speed up mail delivery.

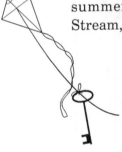

DO IT: Innovation and Invention, Part Three
You've already made observations, developed some hypotheses to explain your observations, and conducted experiments to find out which (if any) of your hypotheses were correct. Now, what can you do with this information? It's time to take action!

Materials
the test results of your experiments in "Innovation and Invention, Part Two"
pencil
sheet of paper

Procedure

1. Look at the results of your experiments. What have you learned?

2. Based on what you now know, list your possibilities for action. For example, if you discovered that the rose blossoms are drooping because the bush is getting too much sun, you might want to move the bush—or build a special roof over the bush, called an arbor, that will let just enough sun through. You might even decide to breed a

more sun-resistant strain of rosebush. Moving the bush is a simple, practical solution. Building your own version of an arbor is an innovative idea. A whole new kind of rosebush is an invention.

3. Pick one possibility on your list to act on. For example, "Build an arbor to let just enough sun through."

4. Draw up a plan for taking action. (Remember, you don't have to build or make something to take action to solve a problem. Your plan may involve talking with people, reorganizing a closet, or even developing a better way to keep your sister out of your room.)

   You will need to start by making a list of the materials you will need (in the case of the arbor, you'll need wood, nails, a hammer, measuring tape, and so on). You may need to add "adult helper" to your list if you are working with sharp objects or electricity. You may also need help to develop a workable design.

   Now list the steps you will take as you complete your plan. In the case of the arbor, you'll probably start with: "Find the money to buy the materials; buy the materials" and so on.

5. Take action! Go ahead and do what you planned to do.

Don't be discouraged if your first attempt at invention or problem solving is not completely successful. Many of the world's greatest inventors, including Ben Franklin, had to experiment with many solutions before they succeeded in solving a problem. Trying, **troubleshooting** (problem solving), and then trying again is an important part of innovating or inventing.

What Next?

If you are like Ben Franklin, you will find that you want to keep questioning and learning. At the end of each chapter, you will find a list of books to help you do that.

The Book of Think (Or How to Solve a Problem Twice Your Size). Marilyn Burns. New York: Little, Brown, 1976.

Gee, Wiz! How to Mix Art and Science or the Art of Thinking Scientifically. Linda Allison and David Katz. New York: Little, Brown, 1983.

47 Easy-to-Do Classic Science Experiments. Eugen F. Provenzo, Jr., and Asterie Baker Provenzo. New York: Dover Publications, 1990.

175 Science Experiments to Amuse and Amaze Your Friends: Experiments! Tricks! Things to Make! Brenda Walpole. New York: Random House, 1991.

Science Experiments Index for Young People. Mary Anne Pilger. Englewood, CO: Libraries Unlimited, Inc., 1988.

Scienceworks: An Ontario Science Centre Book of Experiments. Tina Holdcroft. Reading, MA: Addison-Wesley, 1986.

The Thomas Edison Book of Easy and Incredible Experiments. The Thomas Alva Edison Foundation. New York: John Wiley & Sons, Inc., 1988.

The Way Things Work. David Macaulay. Boston, MA: Houghton Mifflin, 1988.

Chapter 2

Exploring the Weather

What is lightning? Why does the temperature of the water in the ocean vary in different places? Why do storms sometimes travel from southwest to northeast, when the wind seems to be blowing in the opposite direction?

Ben Franklin wanted to understand what makes weather, and he looked for answers wherever and whenever he could. To learn more about weather, he paid attention to the wind, the clouds, the temperature of water and air, and the patterns of storms. He asked questions about what he saw—and then he did his best to answer them.

Sometimes Franklin went to great trouble to watch the weather. On one famous occasion, he flew a kite into a storm to learn more about storms and lightning. Another time, in Maryland, he chased a whirlwind for miles on horseback. He tried to break the whirlwind with his whip, until it moved out of reach into the branches of the trees. And while sailing across the Atlantic Ocean, he measured the temperature of the water every day. He even asked his friends to report on the weather in their home colonies for him.

Franklin wasn't always able to answer his questions about the weather. Quite often, his answers were wrong. Many of his questions weren't answered until the twentieth century and the invention of the satellite. It was only when people could see the Earth from space that they could see the huge weather patterns that affect our world.

(NASA)

22

Even though he didn't always have the right answers, Franklin's questions were important in our understanding of weather. When investigating Franklin's questions, modern **meteorologists** (scientists who study the weather) have learned a great deal about how the weather works.

Watching the Weather

Take a sheet of paper and colored pencils and try to draw a cloud. Don't look out the window! Chances are, your cloud looked like this:

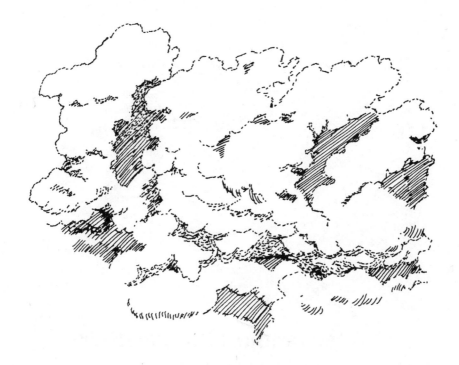

Most of the time we think of clouds as fluffy and white. Now look out the window or step outside. Do the clouds really look like your drawing? You may see fluffy, white clouds. But you may also notice long, streaky clouds, or even little scattered clouds. Maybe the sky is overcast, and all you can see is a white or gray ceiling.

Now take your paper and pencils outside and draw a picture of the sky. To do this, you'll have to observe many things. For instance, you'll have to notice which clouds are high and which are low. You'll have to notice all the different kinds of clouds and their locations and shapes. You'll also have to notice whether different clouds are different colors.

There is a great deal to notice about the weather, and clouds are only one part of the story. Even without special instruments, you can notice many things. For instance:

- What is the temperature? Is it hot? Comfortable? Cold? Jot down your answer to this question on your cloud drawing.

- Is it raining? Damp? Foggy? Dry? Jot this answer down, too.

- How strong is the wind, and in what directions is it blowing? Watch the clouds in order to answer these questions. Now put arrows on your drawing to indicate the direction in which the wind is moving the clouds.

- Look at your drawing. By noticing the weather and putting your observations on paper, you have taken a big step toward understanding **meteorology** (the science of weather).

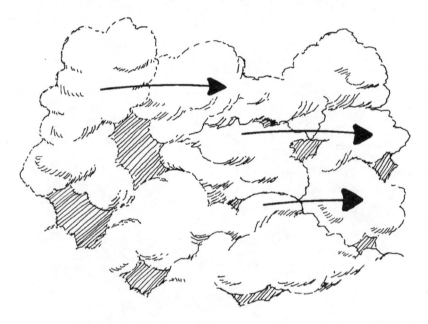

Understanding the Weather

When you step outside and notice the weather, you are really observing the mass of air that is in your region right now. As that mass of air is pushed aside by another mass, the weather changes. Meteorologists (scientists who study weather) use both simple and sophisticated instruments to observe the process of change, and to predict the kind of weather the next air mass will bring.

Masses of air are affected by three important things:

- Where the air mass has come from (if it has come from the north pole, the mass will probably be cold).

- Where the air mass has been on its journey to your neighborhood (if it has crossed the ocean, the mass will probably carry more water than if it has crossed the desert).

Where the air mass is going (the direction of the wind is very important to the progress of weather systems).

When air moves over warm parts of the Earth, it picks up heat. When it moves over cold parts, it becomes colder. The movement and mixing of warm and cold air masses is an important part of the Earth's weather system.

Meteorological instruments record information about the air mass around them. Some are able to detect changes as one air mass is pushed aside and another moves in. The instruments you will build are simple versions of instruments meteorologists use around the world.

Building a Weather Station

Build your own weather station to track the weather, as Ben Franklin did. Your eyes are an important tool for observation, but here is how to make six instruments that will help you observe and forecast the weather.

With your weather instruments, you will be noticing **relative changes**—that is, changes that are compared to earlier changes. You will use the instruments to answer questions like these:

- Is this afternoon hotter or colder than this morning? (thermometer).

- Does the air contain more water than yesterday? (hygrometer).

- How much water has fallen this month? (rain catcher).

- Is the wind picking up speed or slowing down? (anemometer).

- In what direction is the wind blowing? (wind vane).

- Has the air pressure increased or decreased? (barometer).

You can start to track the movement of weather systems by observing changes in the air mass right over your head. Then, combine your own weather-watching results with information about other locations. You can collect this information from the satellite pictures on television, the weather maps in the newspaper, and up-to-the-minute forecasts on the radio. That way, you will be able to tell what kind of weather is on its way to your neighborhood.

The weather station you are about to build will help you become a better weather watcher. If you decide you are very interested in meteorology, you will probably want to buy some commercially made weather instruments. You can also buy or borrow books about the weather. You may even want to get in touch with national and international weather services. The "What Next?" section at the end of this chapter will give you the information you need to continue learning about meteorology.

Find a safe, outdoor place for your weather station—a spot where you can set up all your instruments so that they will not be disturbed. Of course, since some of your instruments will not be waterproof, you will have to bring them indoors when it rains. Read this chapter and gather your materials. Now, you are ready to build your own weather station!

Measuring Hot and Cold

Thermometers are instruments that measure temperature—hot and cold. You already know that temperature is part of the weather: it tells you whether you should be wearing short sleeves, a jacket, or a warm coat. You probably also know that temperature can affect the weather. For instance, you're more likely to get snow in cold weather and thunderstorms in hot weather.

Over most of the Earth, temperatures change with the seasons. As our part of the Earth tilts away from the sun, we get colder, and it is winter. When our part of the Earth tilts toward the sun, we get warmer, and it is summer.

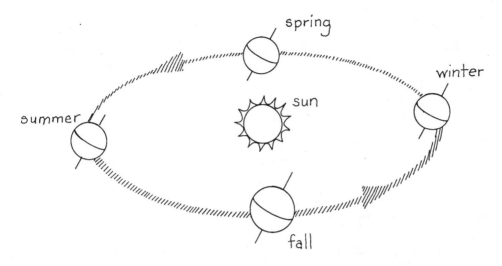

To read changes in temperature, properly, you will need to buy a thermometer. But if you are interested in making your own thermometer, just to see how a thermometer works, here's how:

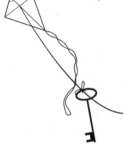

MAKE IT: Thermometer

Materials
tap water
rubbing alcohol (*Caution:* do not drink this!)
clear, narrow-necked plastic bottle (11-ounce (0.75-liter) water
    bottles work well.)
food coloring
clear plastic drinking straw
modeling clay

Procedure

1. Pour equal parts of tap water and rubbing alcohol into the bottle, filling it about ⅛ of the way up.

2. Add a few drops of food coloring and mix well.

3. Place the straw in the bottle. (*Caution:* do not drink from the straw!) Dip the straw into the water, but don't let it touch the bottom.

4. Seal the neck of the bottle with the modeling clay so that the straw stands upright. Hold your hands on the bottle, and watch what happens to the liquid in the straw.

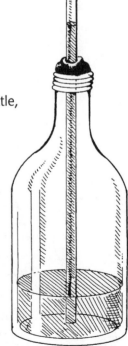

Congratulations! You have built an alcohol thermometer!
Like a store-bought thermometer, the chemicals you used in your

thermometer expanded as they warmed up. The expanding alcohol no longer fit into the bottom of the bottle. So, as the alcohol expanded, it moved up the straw. If you had overheated your alcohol thermometer, the liquid would have poured out the top of the straw.

Experiment with your thermometer. Does it register colder temperatures at certain times of day? Does the wind make the temperature colder? Do sunlight and shadow affect temperature? If your homemade thermometer can't give you the answers you need, use the thermometer you bought for more accurate readings.

Measuring Air Pressure

Wind is the movement of air. Since air is invisible most of the time, you may think air isn't really anything at all. But if you're a runner or a bike rider, you know air is real. You can feel the air as you push your way through it.

Like many other things, if you push on air, it squashes down. If there is no room for the air to squash *out*ward, it will get packed tighter and tighter. Air pressure is the force exerted on the air in the atmosphere. The air will be under great **pressure,** or force. Air blown into a balloon is under pressure. The more air you blow, into the balloon, the more the air is packed inside the balloon's rubber skin. When you release the neck of the balloon, the air inside rushes out and returns to the lower pressure of the air in the rest of the room.

High air pressure in the atmosphere acts like the high-pressure air in the balloon. It always moves toward lower-pressure air. This movement is one of the most important causes of wind.

A **barometer** is an instrument that measures changes in air pressure. An air mass under high pressure acts in certain ways—for instance, in the northern hemisphere, winds in a high-pressure area travel **clockwise** (in the same direction as the hands of a clock) and down in the center. High-pressure air masses tend to bring sunny weather. Of course, if the high-pressure air has traveled from the north, it may bring *cold* sunny weather.

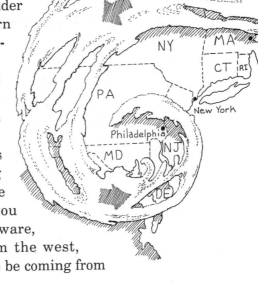

An air mass that is under low pressure acts differently from an air mass under high pressure. First, in the southern hemisphere, winds travel **counterclockwise** (in the opposite direction as the hands of a clock) and up in the center. When a low-pressure system moves in, you're likely to see overcast skies or rain.

Although the wind in an air mass makes a big circle, the circle is so big you can't feel it from your spot on the ground. Look at the picture and you will see, for example, that in Delaware, the wind seems to be coming from the west, whereas in Philadelphia, it seems to be coming from the east.

DO IT: Discover Air Pressure

It may be hard for you to believe that air—which feels like nothing—can change the weather. If so, try this activity to prove to yourself how strong air really is!

Materials
clear plastic drinking glass
tap water
index card big enough to cover the top of the glass
You must have access to a sink.

Procedure

1. Fill the glass to the brim with tap water.

2. Place the index card over the glass. Be sure the top of the glass is completely covered.

3. Standing over the sink, hold the card against the glass as you turn the glass upside down.

4. Let go of the card.

Why didn't the water pour out of the glass? The water stayed in the glass because the air pressure against the card was stronger than **gravity** (the force of attraction that causes objects to fall to the center of the earth) pulling the card down. After a while, though, water will soak into the card. The card will become too heavy, and gravity will overcome the air pressure. The card will fall off the glass, and the water will pour into the sink.

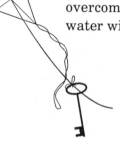

MAKE IT: Barometer

Is the air above us under higher pressure or lower pressure than it was yesterday? Is the pressure changing fast? A barometer can give you the answers to these questions—and help you predict weather changes.

If the air pressure is falling, a low-pressure air mass is on its way. The wind moving over your area blows counterclockwise, and rain may be coming. If the air pressure is rising, a high-pressure air mass is moving in, and fair skies are likely.

Materials

scissors
round balloon
wide-mouthed glass jar
rubber band
plastic drinking straw
transparent tape
index card

Procedure

1. Cut off the neck of the balloon.

2. Stretch the balloon around the jar very tightly, pulling the end of the balloon off to the side so the surface is flat. Wrap the rubber band around the balloon and jar to keep the balloon from slipping.

3. Cut one end of the straw to form a point.

cut here

4. With a small piece of tape, attach the uncut end of the straw to the center of the balloon.

5. Push down lightly on the balloon, and watch what happens to the end of the straw. By pushing down on the balloon, you imitated an increase in air pressure.

6. Put your barometer in a safe place. It doesn't have to be outside. Tape the index card to the wall next to the barometer. The straw should come to about the middle of the card.

7. Mark the card where the straw points. Write the date and time next to your mark.

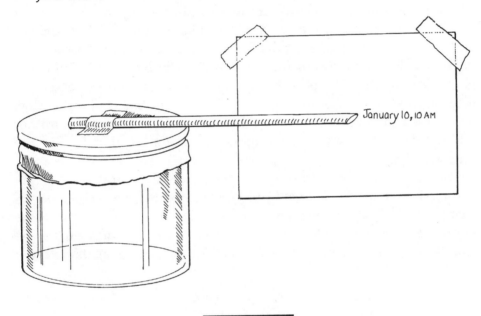

January 10, 10 AM

Greater air pressure creates greater pressure on your balloon. Like your finger pushing down on the balloon, high-pressure weather systems will make your arrow rise.

By the position of the straw, you will be able to tell whether the air pressure is rising or falling. In order to know if the barometer is rising or falling, you'll need to keep track of the air pressure by marking the card every day. If you fill up the card, tape a second one next to the first one.

If you notice that your arrow is consistently rising over the course of a day or several days, you can predict that a high-pressure system is on the way. This means that fair skies are approaching.

Measuring Wind Direction and Speed

Wind, as you now know, is related to the movement of air from high-pressure to low-pressure areas. Without wind, weather systems would not move around the globe. To find out about wind strength and direction, meteorologists use special tools. You will build a **wind vane,** an instrument to gauge the direction of the wind.

When you are measuring wind direction and speed in just one place, it's hard to see large wind patterns. But you can learn about large weather patterns from national newspapers or television. You can also communicate with friends in other areas by phone, fax, E-mail, or even regular mail. By paying close attention, you may be able to see for yourself that winds travel clockwise around high-pressure areas, and counterclockwise around low-pressure areas. Just by talking to friends in different colonies, Ben Franklin discovered that winds and storms do not move in the same direction.

One night, Ben and his brother were planning to watch an eclipse of the moon at 9:00 P.M. Ben was in Philadelphia, and his brother was in Boston. Ben was disappointed when a storm blew up in Philadelphia, blocking his view of the eclipse. Since the storm was accompanied by winds from the northeast, Ben was sure that his brother, too, had missed the beginning of the eclipse. But a letter from his brother told him that the storm did not arrive in Boston until well after the eclipse had begun.

Ben asked friends in other colonies when they first sighted the storm. He "found the beginning to be always later the farther northeastward. . . ." Although he didn't yet fully understand the circular motion of winds, Franklin was the first to realize that northeast storms begin in the southwest—a surprising and confusing discovery!

MAKE IT: Wind Vane

A wind vane is a simple tool that tells you the direction of the wind. It can be helpful for predicting weather, since most weather is carried by wind.

Materials

pencil
index card
scissors
2 hollow coffee stirrers
paper clip
ruler

pushpin
plastic drinking straw
modeling clay
sheet of plain paper
compass

Procedure

1. Trace or draw the wind-vane pattern onto the index card.

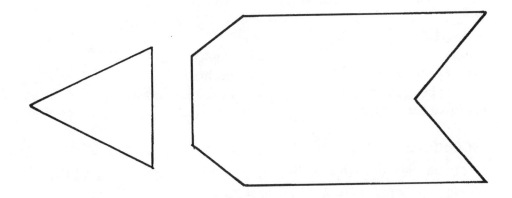

2. Cut out two pieces of the pattern.
3. Cut a slit at each end of the first stirrer. Insert the two pieces of the pattern into the slits to form an arrow, which is the "vane."

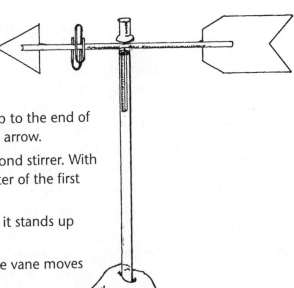

4. To balance the vane, attach the paper clip to the end of the stirrer that is holding the point of the arrow.
5. Cut a 1.5-inch (4-cm) piece from the second stirrer. With the pushpin, attach this piece to the center of the first stirrer.
6. Push the straw into the modeling clay so it stands up straight.
7. Push the short stirrer into the straw so the vane moves freely. You now have a wind vane!
8. Set your wind vane on the sheet of paper. Use the

compass to find north. Then mark off north, south, east, and west with the ruler. For more accuracy, you can also mark off northeast, northwest, southeast, and southwest.

════════════

Your wind vane will tell you the direction in which the wind is traveling. For example, if the vane points north, the wind is traveling toward the north. You will be able to track the wind over time by recording your observations on the chart at the end of the chapter.

MAKE IT: Anemometer

Your wind vane tells you in which direction the wind is blowing. An **anemometer** is an instrument that measures the speed of the wind. These two pieces of information about the wind—direction and speed—help meteorologists identify storms and other weather patterns.

Materials

scissors
4 small paper cups
marking pen (any color)
2 strips of corrugated cardboard

stapler
pushpin
pencil with eraser
modeling clay

Procedure

1. Cut off the rolled edges of the paper cups to make the cups lighter.

2. Color the outside of one cup with the marking pen.

3. Cross the cardboard strips so they look like a plus sign (+). Staple them together.

4. Staple the cups to the ends of the cardboard strips, making sure that all the cups face the same direction. You have made an anemometer.

5. With the pushpin, attach the center of the anemometer to the eraser end of the pencil. Blow on the anemometer to make sure it spins freely.

6. Place the modeling clay on a surface, such as a rock or table top. Stick the sharp end of the pencil into the clay.

7. To take anemometer readings, hold the anemometer up to your eyes and count the number of times the colored cup passes by in a minute. You will measure wind speeds in turns per minute.

Professional meteorologists convert turns per minute to miles (kilometers) per hour, but this is not necessary for your weather watching.

———

Read your anemometer at different times of day, or in different places. Do the readings change? Can you feel the difference in wind speed on your skin? Do faster wind speeds move the clouds along faster?

Measuring the Water in the Air

Humidity is a measure of water vapor in the air. A weather report that says, "We are at 20 percent relative humidity" means the air is holding 20 percent of the amount of water vapor it is able to hold at that particular temperature.

Water in the air falls as rain, snow, sleet, and hail. Water vapor in the air can make a hot summer day muggy, or a cool morning foggy. Many materials soak up water vapor. Doors stick on humid days because the wood expands, and even your hair soaks up water—that's why humid weather can make your hair limp.

Ben Franklin was among the first to notice the effect of humidity on certain materials. He noticed that wooden boxes on ships shrank in Philadelphia, but actually swelled in England. He understood that the wood expanded because it soaked up a lot of water in England's very damp climate. Ben realized that expanding materials can measure humidity. Based on his observations of the wooden boxes, he even came up with an idea for a meteorological instrument to measure humidity.

The **hygrometer** (instrument to measure the amount of humidity in the air) you are about to make is based on Franklin's discovery that certain materials soak up water on humid days. The material you will use is a strand of your own hair. Your hygrometer will tell you whether the amount of water in the air is increasing or decreasing.

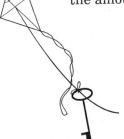

MAKE IT: Hygrometer

Materials

paper hole-punch
2 index cards
scissors
brass paper fastener

strand of your hair
ruler
masking tape
pencil

Procedure

1. Punch a hole in the first index card about halfway down the short edge of the card and 1 inch (2.5 cm) in from the edge.

2. Cut a thin strip lengthwise from the second index card. The strip

should be slightly wider than the hole you punched. Cut one end of the strip to form a point. Punch a hole in the other end.

3. With the brass fastener, attach the unpointed end of the strip to the hole in the first index card.

4. Pull out a strand of hair at least 4 inches (10 cm) long. Tape one end of the strand to the pointed end of the strip.

5. Tape the other end of the hair strand to the top of the card (or to the back, if it reaches over). The pointed strip should hang in the middle of the card.

6. Mark the card where the pointed end of the strip hangs.

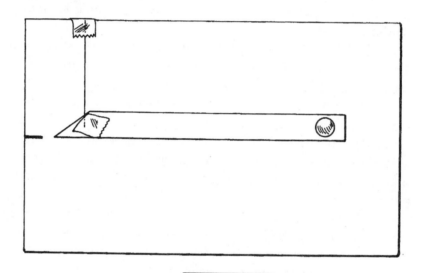

To use your hair hygrometer, place it outside with the rest of your weather-station instruments. Every morning, mark the position of the strip to see whether it rises and falls with changes in humidity.

Your hair soaks up water in the air. The more water in the air, the more water in your hair! You'll find that the hair strand in your hygrometer becomes straighter and longer when it is full of water. As the hair strand lengthens, the arrow falls. So, the greater the relative humidity, the longer the hair—and the lower the arrow points. Of course, different kinds of hair will produce different results in your hygrometer. Try using very curly hair, very straight hair, animal hair, or even synthetic hair to see what happens.

MAKE IT: Rain Catcher
Too much rain causes severe flooding—like the overflow of the Mississippi River in the summer of 1993. Too little rain results in droughts, causing crops to wither and die.

How much rain falls in your area? How much rain is too much? How much is too little? The rain catcher you will make will help you measure the rainfall in your area. You can compare the amount of rain you catch to the amount of rain your area usually gets. Many encyclopedias contain information about average regional rainfall. Monthly rainfall averages are often reported in newspapers and on televised weather reports.

Materials
masking tape
clear, narrow tube with a flat bottom, sealed at one end (Jewelry beads
    come in this kind of tube.)
ruler
pencil
lump of clay

Procedure

1. Attach a strip of tape the entire length of the narrow tube, from top to bottom.

2. To **calibrate** (mark with a standard of measurement) the tube for inches, lay the ruler against the masking tape on the tube. Mark off "1 inch," "2 inches," and so on, until you reach the top of the tube. To calibrate the tube for centimeters, measure and mark off centimeters on the masking tape.

3. To make a secure base for your rain catcher, push the bottom of the tube into the lump of clay. Flatten the bottom of the lump so that the tube can stand up straight.

4. Place the tube outdoors to collect rainfall.

5. After a rainfall, record how many inches or centimeters of rain fell by checking the height of the rain against the measurements on the tube.

Cloud Watching

Meteorological instruments are important ways to observe and predict the weather. But your instruments can't do everything. The shapes, sizes, colors, and movements of clouds can tell you a great deal about the weather. None of your instruments can tell you about cloud formations, so you will have to use your eyes and your experience to interpret what you observe in the sky.

Clouds carry rain, and you know that different kinds of clouds can be expected to appear in different kinds of weather. You create a mini-cloud when you breathe out on a cold day. But just what is a cloud?

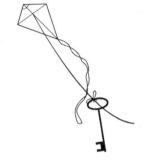

DO IT: A Cloud in a Jar

To find out more about how clouds form, try this experiment:

Materials

piece of chalk
newspaper
hammer
nail
2 lids: one that fits the jar,
  and one that's extra large
  for the jar

medium-sized jelly or pickle
  jar
very hot tap water
timer
2 ice cubes
adult helper

Procedure

1. Place the piece of chalk on the newspaper. Ask your adult helper to hit the chalk with the hammer to make fine, powdery chalk dust. Set the chalk dust aside.

2. Ask your adult helper to punch holes in the extra-large jar lid, using the hammer and nail.

3. Fill the jar with very hot tap water, and cover it with the lid that fits. Let the jar stand for about 2 minutes.

4. Remove the lid, and pour out about 90 percent of the water.

5. Place the extra-large lid with the holes in it on top of the jar. Put the ice cubes on the lid. Let the jar stand for about 3 minutes.

6. Remove the ice cubes and the extra-large lid.

7. Sprinkle a pinch of chalk dust into the jar. Cover the jar tightly with the lid that fits.

8. After about 2 minutes, observe the inside of the jar. A cloud has formed!

═══════════

By heating and then cooling the water in the jar, you caused droplets of water to form. As this experiment shows, clouds are collections of tiny water droplets that form around particles of dust, dirt, or salt. Without the chalk dust, you would not have seen a cloud in the jar. Without tiny particles in the air, we would not have clouds—or rain.

Cloud Formations

On many days you can see several different kinds of clouds. The five most common types of clouds are:

Cirrus clouds: feathery wisps, curls, or ringlets, high in the sky. These clouds often mean fair skies.

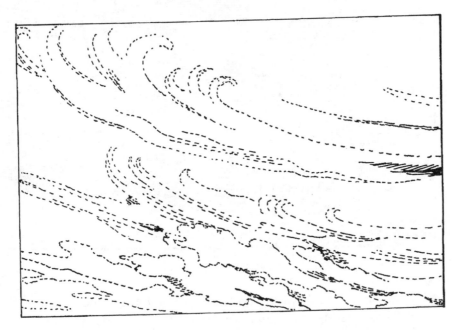

Altocumulus clouds: fluffy, heaped-up masses of clouds at midlevel. These clouds may mean changing weather.

Nimbus clouds: low, dark-gray clouds, full of water. These clouds generally mean it is raining or snowing, or that rain or snow is on the way.

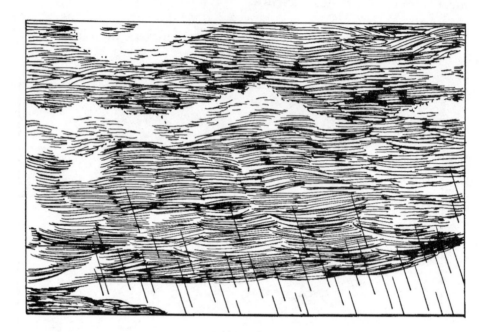

Stratus clouds: calm, flat layers of clouds that spread out at a low level. These clouds may mean an overcast day or approaching rain or snow.

Cumulus clouds: puffy and bunched-up clouds at a low level. These clouds often mean fair weather.

Clouds are part of weather systems. By watching clouds, you will be better able to predict the weather. Remember, though, clouds can change quickly—and they may mean more than one thing.

Look outside right now. Can you name the types of clouds you see? Are low, dark nimbus clouds blowing toward you—the kind that often mean rain or snow is on the way? Do you see high, light cirrus clouds in a blue sky? Just by looking at the clouds, and noting the wind direction, you can make some intelligent guesses about the kind of weather that is coming.

You can record your cloud observations on the chart in the next section. Look at the sample forecast to see how cloud observations play an important part in weather prediction.

Tracking the Weather

Congratulations! With your new weather station, you are now a full-fledged weather watcher. With the instruments you have built, you will be able to keep track of changes in the atmosphere, and make some predictions about the weather that will be coming to your region.

Look at the weather instruments you have built. Some, like the wind vane and the rain catcher, will give you very specific information. With these instruments, you will be able to tell people that the wind is coming from the west, or that 2 inches (5 cm) of rain fell this month.

But some of your instruments will give you only relative information. For instance, your anemometer will tell you that today is windier than yesterday was—but it will not tell you how many miles (kilometers) an hour the wind is blowing.

In meteorology, relative information is as important as specific information. In fact, weather changes over time are often more important than a "snapshot" of weather conditions at a specific moment in time.

For your weather station to be useful, you need to keep track of information. By carefully recording changes in air pressure, wind speed, and so forth, you will be able to chart **trends** (the direction in which events seem to be moving) in the weather. Your understanding of these trends will help you make forecasts.

Another useful way to track the weather is to work with friends who live in different parts of your region. Have everyone in your weather group take a reading at the same time of day. Then, share your information by phone, fax, E-mail, or regular mail. By finding out where a storm first hit, or where the barometer first dropped, you can begin to build a picture of a weather system.

To track your weather readings, you will need a chart like this one. Each day, at the same time, check your instruments, check the sky, and enter your observations on the chart. On the first day, you'll have to mark the index card or sheet of paper near your instruments. That mark will be your starting point. After the first day, you'll be able to tell whether your barometer has risen or fallen, whether your hygrometer has risen or fallen, and so on. Don't forget to mark the card or paper every day.

Sample Weather-Tracking Chart and Forecast

	Monday	Tuesday	Wednesday	Thursday	Friday
Temperature (in degrees)	30	25	28	32	30
Barometer	Mark card	Rises	No change	Dropping	Dropping
Anemometer (turns per minute)	6	3	0–1	1–3	3–4
Wind vane	East	Northeast	Changing	South	South
Hygrometer	Mark card	Lower	No change	Rising	Rising
Clouds	Scattered	Clearer	Mostly clear	High clouds	Overcast

In this example, an air mass is moving quickly through the area. Another air mass replaces it very quickly. In real life, weather does not always change this fast. Sometimes, high- or low-pressure air masses stay in one place for days.

In some parts of the country, for example, the Southwest, the

weather may stay the same for weeks. If you live in a region of the country where there is little change in the weather, try taking readings twice a day—at about 8:00 to 9:00 A.M. and at about 4:00 to 6:00 P.M. You will find that your readings change a great deal depending upon the time of day.

If you were to obtain readings like the ones here, you might post the following forecasts on your refrigerator:

Monday: You won't be able to make a prediction the first day you use your weather station, because you won't know what changes have occurred since yesterday.

Tuesday: Expect sunnier skies and drier conditions. A high-pressure air mass is probably approaching.

Wednesday: A high-pressure air mass is centered overhead. Expect sunny skies.

Thursday: The high-pressure air mass is leaving. A low-pressure air mass may be approaching. Expect fair skies today, but storms may be coming in the next few days.

Friday: A low-pressure air mass is approaching or is overhead. Expect a period of clouds and rain.

Don't worry if your forecasts aren't right some of the time. Even professional meteorologists can't predict the weather correctly all the time. Weather is constantly changing, and even a small change in wind direction can make a big difference in the weather ahead. That's what makes weather forecasting interesting—and that's what makes it frustrating, even for meteorologists.

Forecasting the Weather

Weather on the Earth is complex. Even with expensive high-tech equipment such as satellites and radar, meteorologists are able to forecast weather only a few days into the future.

To prove to yourself how hard it is to forecast weather, copy a five-day weather forecast for your region from a newspaper, television news, or a weather channel. Now, record the actual weather for the five days. How accurate was the forecast?

Since you don't have fancy equipment to track weather, predicting the weather for more than a day into the future will be hard. Sometimes, you'll be able to predict the weather only a few hours ahead. Your records will help you to forecast the weather—and so will your observations, your common sense, and your television or newspaper report. Here is how to do it:

1. *Tracking trends.* If the weather has been hot and dry for a whole month, chances are tomorrow will be hot and dry. If the temperature has been dropping steadily, it's a good guess that tomorrow's temperature will continue to fall.

2. *Watching your instruments and the sky.* As low-pressure systems approach your weather station, the wind will probably blow harder, and the barometer will fall. You are also likely to see clouds approaching. When you see these signs, you can be pretty sure a storm is on the way.

3. *Using common sense.* Instruments and observations are important when forecasting weather, but so is common sense. In summer, most forecasters don't predict snow—and in winter it's unlikely you'll have a prediction of a hot, muggy day!

4. *Using television and newspapers.* You might not have access to your own satellite, but television stations do. Tune in to the news or weather channel and study the satellite images. The information you obtain from these images will help you interpret your own findings.

Ben Franklin used all of his resources to learn about the weather. Although he didn't have television or a satellite, he had plenty of curiosity, common sense, friends, and certain instruments to help him. And, even without a satellite, he made discoveries that changed the way we think about the weather—and the world around us.

What Next?

Your homemade weather station is a good way to get started in meteorology. But if the field excites you, you'll probably want to find more information about it. Here are some books you can read and places you can write for more information about meteorology:

Sources of Weather Information

American Meteorological Society
1701 K Street NW, Suite 300
Washington, DC 20006

National Climatic Data Center
Federal Building
Asheville, NC 28801

National Weather Service Public Affairs Office
1325 East-West Highway
Silver Spring, MD 20910

Weather Reading

Weatherwise, a bimonthly magazine
Heldref Publications
1319 18th Street NW
Washington, DC 20036

The Big Storm. Bruce Hiscock. New York: Atheneum, 1993.
Cloudy with a Chance of Meatballs. Judi Barrett. New York, Aladdin Books, 1982.
The Reasons for Seasons: The Great Cosmic Megagalactic Trip Without Moving From Your Chair. Linda Allison. New York: Little, Brown, 1975.
The Sierra Club Book of Weather Wisdom. Vicki McVey. New York: Sierra Club/Little, Brown, 1991.
Weather: Air Masses, Clouds, Rainfall, Storms, Weather Maps, and Climate. Paul Lehr et al., New York: Simon & Schuster, 1957.
The Weather Book. Jack Williams. New York: Vintage Books, 1992.
Weather. Pierre Kohler. New York: Barron's, 1985.

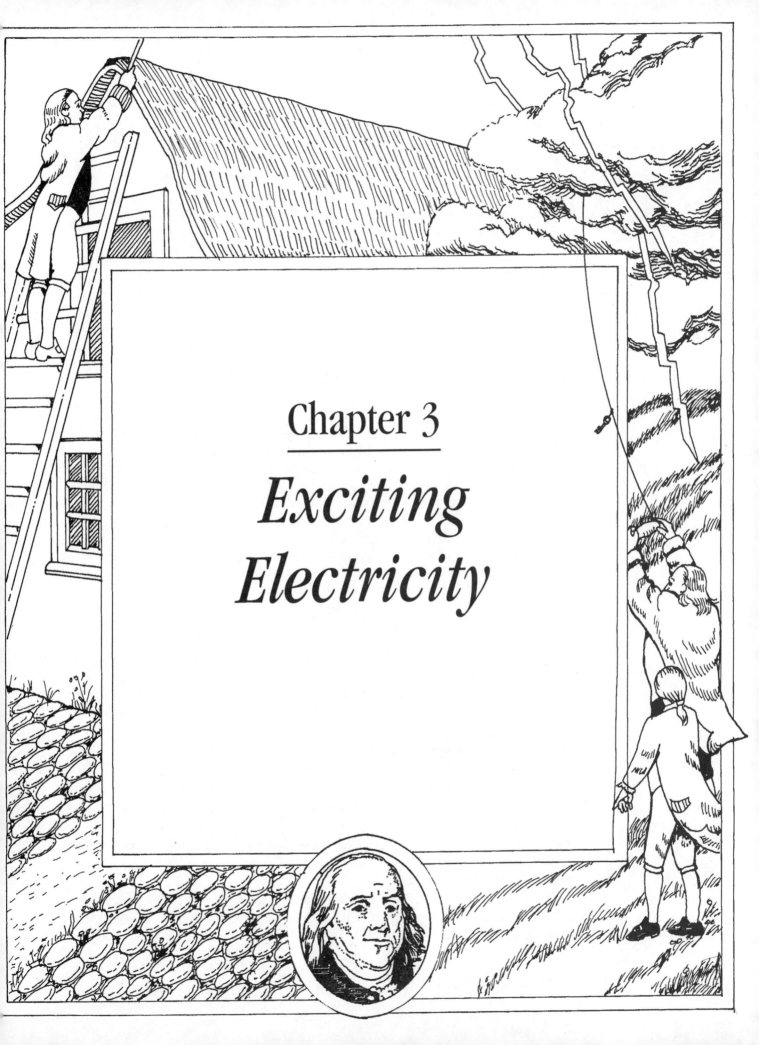

Chapter 3

Exciting Electricity

It was spring, 1752. Scientists in Europe and America were fascinated by electricity—a strange power that could create painful shocks, move objects, and make sparks fly out of a person's fingers. Like the other scientists of his time, Ben Franklin was interested in electricity, and he conducted a number of experiments with **static electricity** (electricity that is not moving in a circuit). Not until his famous kite-and-key experiment, however, did Franklin's interest in electricity become internationally known.

Franklin wanted to prove that lightning and electricity are the same thing. To do this, he first made a kite out of a silk handkerchief and two sticks. Then, he attached to the kite a long string made of hemp (a kind of twine). Near the end of the string, he tied a silk ribbon, and to that ribbon he tied a key. Then, he waited for a storm. Joseph Priestley, a friend of Ben's, told the story like this:

> . . . he took the opportunity of the first approaching thunderstorm to take a walk in the fields, in which there was a shed convenient for his purpose. But, dreading the ridicule which too commonly attends unsuccessful attempts in science, he communicated his intended experiment to nobody but his son who assisted him in raising the kite.
>
> The kite being raised, a considerable time elapsed before there was any appearance of its being electrified. One very promising cloud had passed over it without any effect, when, at length, just as he was beginning to despair of his contrivance, he observed some loose threads of the hempen string to stand erect and to avoid one another. . . . Struck with this promising appearance, he immediately presented his knuckle to the key and . . . the discovery was complete. He perceived a very evident electric spark.

Franklin had proved, along with French scientists of the time, that lightning and electricity are the same thing. The experiment was dangerous, although Franklin didn't know it then—the lightning could easily have killed him! Ben's discovery led to many inventions, the first of which was the **lightning rod,** a long metal pole that attracts lightning away from houses and leads it into the ground.

But Franklin's discoveries about electricity went far beyond lightning. At the time Franklin was conducting his experiments, people believed there were two kinds of electricity. They thought one kind attracted objects, and the other kind pushed away objects. Franklin was able to prove that this wasn't so. This discovery was the first step toward the invention of the battery, the electric motor, and the alternating electrical current used everywhere today.

In the next sections of this chapter, you'll read more about positive and negative charges—and you will conduct some of your own experiments and activities.

Discovering Electricity

Electricity is everywhere. To prove the truth of this statement, make an inventory of the way you use electricity during your day. Start by listing the electrical appliances you use. Then, list the ways you use electricity as you engage in activities, such as reading, eating, and traveling to and from school. How does your body use electricity to think, sense, and move? (*Hint:* check Chapter 4, "Making Music," for information about electricity and your body.)

How important is electricity in your life? Now that you have listed the many ways you use electricity every day, try to spend a day without using electricity. Pick a day when you can organize your own time—a Saturday, Sunday, or vacation day. Each time you use electricity—for example, phoning a friend, turning on a light, or toasting your bread—give yourself one point. Were you able to get through the day with fewer than ten points? If you like, share this activity with a friend—see who can do a better job of not using electricity for a day. You might find it's harder than you think!

Understanding Electricity

Although Ben Franklin experimented with electricity, only much later did scientists begin to understand the causes of electricity. Scientists had a problem explaining electricity because, while electricity itself can be seen, heard, and felt, the reason for its existence is not obvious to any of our senses. Electricity puzzled scientists because the process of electricity happens at an **atomic** level. This means that electricity is related to atoms—tiny particles of matter that make up everything we know on Earth. Explaining the causes of electricity, then, awaited the scientists of the twentieth century.

Eventually, it was discovered that atoms are made up of even tinier particles, called **electrons,** which have a negative charge and move around the central portions of atoms. The **nucleus,** or central portion, of an atom contains positively charged particles, called **protons.** When an atom contains more electrons than protons, it is **negatively charged;** when it contains more protons than electrons, it is **positively charged.** When an atom has as many negative electrons as positive protons, it is **neutral,** or holds no electrical charge.

Electricity occurs as electrons move from atom to atom. There are lots of ways to do this. In a thunderstorm, many electrons build up in the bottom of a cloud, until they suddenly jump to the ground. You can get electrons to move with a rotating magnet (that's what a generator does), or you can do it with a chemical reaction—what a battery does.

Static Electricity

You work with electricity every day. From light bulbs to brain impulses, you are constantly interacting with electricity in one way or another. But, as you probably know, experimenting with the electrical system in your home is very dangerous. So *never* tinker with electrical sockets or electrical appliances. How, then, can you conduct experiments with electricity?

When Ben Franklin conducted his experiments, he did not work with electrical wires, power stations, or transformers. He worked with static electricity. Static simply means "not moving"—so static electricity, as you learned earlier, is electricity that is not moving. It's the kind of electricity that gives you a small shock when you touch a doorknob after walking across a carpeted floor. You can also create static electricity by rubbing a balloon against a carpet or your hair. Then, watch the balloon stick to your head or to the wall. Static electricity has some interesting and unexpected properties—interesting enough to keep many scientists very busy for several hundred years!

Opposites Attract

You have been reading about electrical charges, but what exactly are they? Before Ben Franklin, scientists believed that there were two kinds of electricity: positive and negative. Ben discovered that there is only one kind of electricity, but that some objects can have more electrons than others, making them positively charged, and objects that carry fewer electrons than others are negatively charged.

Positive and negative charges are important for many reasons—but they can also be a lot of fun. Here are ways you can rediscover positive and negative charges for yourself, while amazing your friends.

MAKE IT: An Electroscope

Detecting electricity can be difficult, since electricity is often invisible and silent. But an **electroscope** is an instrument that can help you find electricity anywhere. It will also help you with the experiments in the rest of this chapter.

Materials

scissors

ruler

piece of corrugated cardboard

paper clip

aluminum foil

plastic comb

balloon

piece of wool cloth (such
    as a mitten or scarf)

timer

Procedure

1. Cut a piece of corrugated cardboard into a 1 × 4-inch (2.5 × 10-cm) rectangle.

2. Bend the paper clip into the shape of a fishhook. This will be your "electrode."

3. Cut the aluminum foil into a ¼ × 4-inch (0.7 × 10-cm) strip.

4. Poke the straight end of the hook through the inside layer of the cardboard, as shown in the diagram.

5. Gently fold the aluminum strip in half, and hang it over the hook. The halves are the "leaves."

6. To test your electroscope:

   a. Rub the comb and the balloon with the piece of wool cloth for about 60 seconds each.

   b. Hold the electroscope by the cardboard, and bring it close to the comb. Then, bring it close to the balloon. Watch what happens to the electroscope's leaves.

   c. Touch the comb, and then bring the electroscope close to it. What happens to the leaves? Try the same experiment, this time touching the balloon.

═══════════

You can produce a static electrical charge by rubbing certain items. Combs and balloons become negatively charged when you rub them with wool. This means that there are more negatively charged electrons on the comb or balloon than there are positively charged protons.

When you brought the charged comb and balloon close to the electroscope's leaves, the extra electrons jumped to the electroscope. Both leaves of the electroscope became negatively charged. Two objects with the same charge (either both negative or both positive) repel each other, and the leaves of the electroscope move apart.

The atoms in your electroscope won't stay charged. The leaves will stay apart until the air around them either adds or subtracts electrons. The leaves move back together when the number of electrons equals the number of protons, and the electroscope is electrically neutral.

If you touch the charged comb or balloon, the static electricity will transfer to your body. The object will no longer be charged, and therefore, it will not affect the electroscope.

With your electroscope, test other objects for static electricity. Use the wool cloth to see which objects become electrically charged.

Incredible "Magic" Feats with Static Electricity

Now that you know how to charge an object—and you can tell whether an object is charged—you can have fun experimenting with static electricity. As you've probably already figured out, some materials can hold a static charge better than others. Hair, for example, is easy to charge. In Franklin's day, many scientists—and magicians—used static electricity to impress audiences around the world. At that time, no one knew much about electricity, so there was no one to explain the science behind the magic.

These "magic" feats will amaze your friends and family, just as static electricity amazed people in Franklin's time. But you will understand the science that is behind the magic. When you perform these amazing tricks, you'll be able to explain why they work.

MAKE IT: 'Lectric Legs

Materials
scissors
3 × 6-inch (7.5 × 15-cm) sheet of notebook paper
ruler
9-inch (23-cm) round balloon
helper

Procedure

1. Cut the sheet of paper into eight narrow strips. Do not cut all the way—leave 3 inches (7.5 cm) at the top. These strips are the "legs" of your spider. The uncut part is the spider's body.

2. Inflate the balloon, and tie the neck closed.

3. Hold the spider against your helper's back with its legs down. Rub the balloon in a downward direction over the spider.

4. Pull the spider off your helper's back. Move the balloon around the spider's legs. Watch what happens!

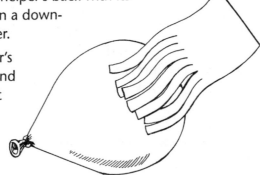

When you rubbed the balloon against the paper spider, you built up static charges on both the balloon and the spider. This happened because protons and electrons separated when you rubbed the balloon against the paper. The charge on the balloon was the opposite of the charge on the spider. Because opposite charges attract each other, the spider's legs were attracted to the balloon. The spider's legs all carried the same charge (either all negative or all positive), so the spider's legs moved away from one another because like charges (the same kind of charges) repel one another.

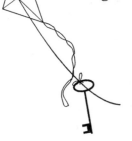

MAKE IT: Moths in Motion

Materials
pencil
sheet of notebook paper
tissue paper
scissors

materials to decorate the moths
   (glue, glitter, marking pens)
small box with plastic lid
wool cloth

Procedure

1. Draw a moth pattern on the sheet of paper, or trace it from the pattern here.

2. Trace four or five moths onto the tissue paper, using your pattern, and cut them out. You may want to color and decorate your moths so they look real.

3. Place the moths in the box, and place the lid on top.

4. With the wool cloth, rub the top of the box in one direction. What happens?

When you rubbed the wool scarf against the plastic lid, an electric charge built up on the lid. The moths inside the box became oppositely charged, and so were attracted to the lid. When the charge on the lid became great enough, the moths were actually pulled up to the lid, and appeared to be jumping. Eventually, the charge will leak away, and the moths will fall back into the box.

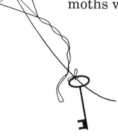

MAKE IT: A Very "Attractive" Comb

Materials

plastic comb
wool scarf or mitten
your electroscope (optional)
You must have access to a sink.

Procedure

1. Turn on the faucet to produce a small stream of water.

2. Rub the comb against the wool scarf or mitten. You may want to use your electroscope to be sure the comb is charged.

3. Hold the comb close to, but not touching, the stream of water. Watch what happens!

The plastic comb became negatively charged when you rubbed it with the wool scarf or mitten. This means there were extra electrons on the comb. The stream of water bent, because each water molecule is pulled toward the charged comb. The atoms in the water were attracted to the extra electrons on the comb.

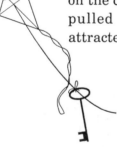

MAKE IT: Dinner-Party Dilemma

This use of static electricity should surprise your friends and family—and make you look like a magician.

Materials

salt
pepper
newspaper
balloon
wool scarf or mitten

Procedure

1. Shake salt and pepper onto the newspaper, and mix them thoroughly.

2. Explain to your audience that there has been an accident. Just before an important dinner party, you spilled the last of the salt and pepper all over the table. Your guests are due, and you have to separate the salt from the pepper before they arrive. Ask your audience if they can think of a way to separate the salt from the pepper.

3. Inflate the balloon, and explain that you will use it to separate the salt from the pepper. Can anyone imagine how you will do this?

4. Rub the balloon with the scarf or mitten.

5. Starting a few inches above the salt and pepper mixture, slowly move the balloon closer and closer to it. What happens?

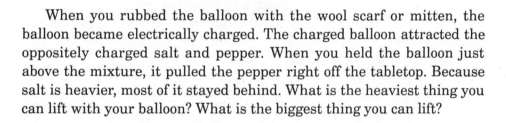

When you rubbed the balloon with the wool scarf or mitten, the balloon became electrically charged. The charged balloon attracted the oppositely charged salt and pepper. When you held the balloon just above the mixture, it pulled the pepper right off the tabletop. Because salt is heavier, most of it stayed behind. What is the heaviest thing you can lift with your balloon? What is the biggest thing you can lift?

Building Electric Machines

So far, you have been amazing your friends with your demonstrations of static electricity—electricity that stands still, and then eventually leaks into the air. Static electricity is fascinating, but it is not especially useful. It can't be used to do work, like run a motor or turn on a light. To do this kind of work, we need electricity that runs continuously, instead of staying in one place.

For electricity to run continuously, it must run around and around in a circle. The circle must be made of certain kinds of materials that carry electricity, called **conductors.** Most metals are good conductors, meaning they carry electricity well, which is why wires are made of metal. The electrical **current,** or flow of electric charge, that runs through household wires operates light bulbs, appliances, and everything else you plug into wall outlets.

A **circuit** is an electrical connection that uses conductive materials to attach an energy source to an electrical appliance and the appliance back to the energy source. Electricity will run around the circuit as long as there is a power source that works to generate energy, and as long as the circuit is complete. If you break the circuit, which is what you do when you turn off a switch, the electricity shuts off.

In this section, you'll build useful machines by using an electric current and circuits. You'll also learn some of the amazing facts about electricity, based on Ben Franklin's work and the work of several other scientists.

Chemistry and Electricity

Ben Franklin's experiments led to the idea that static electricity may have a positive or a negative charge. This useful discovery allowed an Italian scientist, Allessandro Volta, to invent the **battery,** a chemical source of electricity. You may recognize the name Volta, since it is the base of the word "**volt**" (as in "high voltage"), which is a measure of electrical power.

Volta believed that if you could separate positively charged and negatively charged particles—and keep them separate—you could connect them with a conductor (such as wire). In this way, Volta reasoned, you could produce electricity anytime you wanted to for as long as you wanted. Volta's battery, which he produced in 1800, was made of silver and zinc discs that were separated by damp fabric pads.

The unique organization of atoms in silver and zinc made Volta's battery work. But because the battery was big, it was inconvenient to use, and it was expensive. In later years, batteries were made by submerging two rods, made of different materials, in a liquid. A chemical reaction in the liquid caused the negatively charged particles to move toward one rod and the positively charged particles to move toward the other rod. Finally, the **dry cell** was invented. This chemical source of electricity works the same way as Volta's battery, but it uses a conductive paste held inside a waterproof case. This is the type of battery we use today, for example, in flashlights and toys.

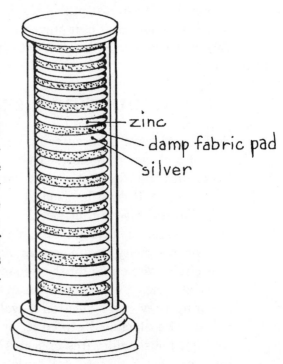

zinc
damp fabric pad
silver

MAKE IT: Sour Circuits

Materials
lemon
knife (to be used by your adult helper)
dime and penny (or zinc strip and copper strip)
adult helper

Procedure

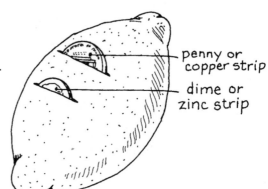

penny or copper strip

dime or zinc strip

1. Roll the lemon back and forth on a table-top and squeeze it lightly to get the juice flowing inside the lemon.

2. Ask your adult helper to cut two slices in the lemon about ½ inch (1 cm) apart, and as wide as the dime or penny.

3. Insert the dime and the penny (or the zinc strip and the copper strip) into the slits in the lemon, as shown in the diagram.

4. With your tongue, touch both coins at once. Do you feel anything?

Acid in the lemon reacted with the metals, pulling positive particles to one metal and negative particles to the other. A small electric current began to flow as a result of this reaction. By placing your tongue on both metals at once, you completed the circuit, allowing the electricity to flow. The sensation you felt on your tongue was caused by the electric current.

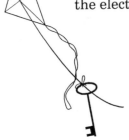

DO IT: Measuring Energy Flow

Materials
thin copper wire
compass
your lemon with its penny and dime

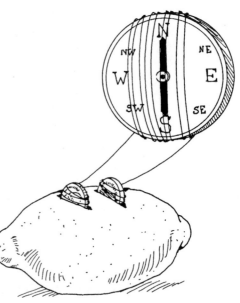

Procedure

1. Wrap the copper wire around the compass.

2. Using the lemon prepared in the "Sour Circuits" experiment above, wind one end of the wire around each coin. Watch the compass needle.

The electric current that was produced traveled through the wire and around the compass. The flow of electricity caused the compass needle to move.

Now that you know something about batteries and circuits, you might want to try some experiments of your own using store-bought batteries, wires (or aluminum foil), and small (flashlight-sized) electric light bulbs. Can you use these materials to build a working circuit? Can your lemon light a small light bulb? Draw a picture of the circuit or circuits you create. (*Caution:* Never open a battery or experiment with batteries of more than 9 volts.)

Magnets and Electricity

Michael Faraday, an English scientist, drew on the work of people like Franklin and Volta to create the first electric motor in 1831. Faraday had discovered yet another source of electricity: the **magnet**—a piece of metal that attracts certain other metals.

For a long time, people were confused about electricity and magnetism. Both are described using the terms "positive" and "negative." (For example, on a magnet, opposite poles attract each other, but like poles **repel** [push away] each other.) At the same time, electricity and magnetism are very different from each other. (For example, electricity can produce sparks, whereas magnetism can lift heavy objects.)

Faraday discovered that if he moved a loop of wire near a magnet, an electric current would pass through the wire. To make the current stronger, he used more loops of wire, and a more powerful magnet. Faraday imagined the magnet's pull as "lines of force" stretching from one end of the magnet to the other. His hypothesis turned out to be a pretty good explanation of how magnets work. As the wire cuts the lines of force, electric current starts to move through the wires.

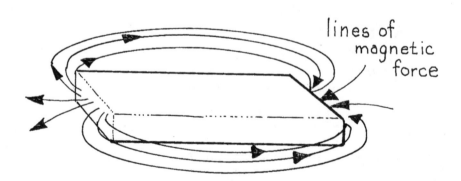

lines of magnetic force

Based on his discovery, Faraday invented a machine called a **generator,** which produces electric power. Electric power can also be used to generate magnetism.

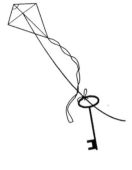

MAKE IT: The Moving Needle

Materials
copper wire
strong scissors or wire cutter
masking tape
compass
bar magnet

Procedure

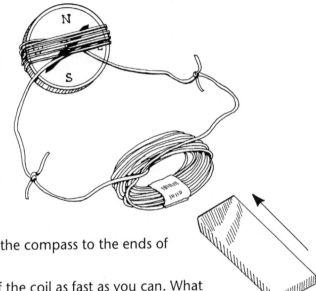

1. Wind the wire 25 times around three fingers, allowing a few inches (centimeters) of free wire at each end.

2. Cut the wire, and tape the coil, so that it stays together.

3. Wind more of the wire around the compass a few times, leaving a few inches (centimeters) of free wire at each end.

4. Connect the ends of the wire from the compass to the ends of the wire from the coil.

5. Move the bar magnet in and out of the coil as fast as you can. What happens to the compass needle?

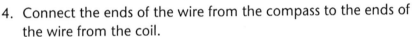

The electric current produced by the magnet and the wire traveled through the wire and around the compass. You might want to try experimenting with different kinds of wire, larger magnets, and so on, to generate more or less electric power.

MAKE IT: Electromagnet

Materials
wire
long nail
strong scissors or wire cutter
battery
masking tape
knife switch (DC, or direct current) available in hardware stores
    or electronic-supply stores

Procedure

1. Wrap the wire tightly around the nail at least 50 times. Cut the wire, leaving a few inches (centimeters) of free wire at each end.

2. Connect one end of the wire to one end of the battery, securing it with the tape. Don't let the tape come between the battery and the wire.

3. Open the knife switch. Connect the other end of the wire to the switch, as in the diagram.

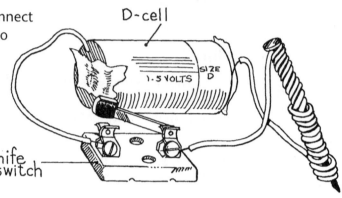

4. Cut another piece of wire, and complete the circuit by connecting one end of the wire to the other end of the battery. Then, connect the other end of the wire to the switch.

5. Close the circuit by closing the switch. You have created an **electromagnet**—a magnet that is created by running electricity through coils of wire wrapped around an iron or steel bar.

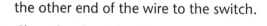

To see how well your electromagnet works, try using it to attract paper clips. How well does it work? What happens when you open the switch? Try experimenting to make your magnet stronger or weaker. Try attracting a whole box of paper clips! What else can you do with your new electromagnet?

MAKE IT: A Motor

Based on his new electromagnet, Faraday invented the **motor**, a machine that harnesses electricity to do work—almost any kind of work. The motor you will build starts the flow of electrons by means of a battery, but you can start the flow in many ways. Can you think of a few ways?

Materials

rubber band
empty coffee can with the lid removed
2 paper clips
2 small horseshoe-shaped magnets
masking tape

3 1-foot (30-cm) pieces of wire
pencil
9-volt battery
piece of thread
scissors

Procedure

1. Stretch the rubber band around the top of the can.

2. Form the paper clips into long S shapes.

3. Turn the magnets so they attract each other. Tape one paper clip to each magnet on the side that does not attract the other magnet.

4. Slip the paper clips under the rubber band so the magnets face each other on opposite sides of the can.

5. Wrap one end of the first piece of wire around the pencil, forming a loop. Slip the pencil out of the loop. Repeat this step for the second piece of wire.

6. Slip the pieces of wire under the rubber band so the tops of the loops are level with the magnets. Hold the wires in place with tape. The long ends of the wires will hang down. You will need them later.

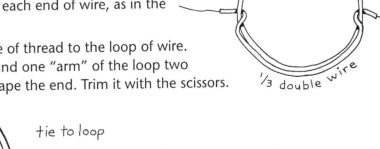

7. Wrap the third piece of wire around the battery. Slip the battery out of the loop, without letting the coil become larger. Tightly loop each end of wire, as in the diagram.

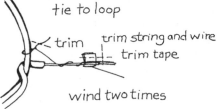

8. Tie the piece of thread to the loop of wire. Wind it around one "arm" of the loop two times, and tape the end. Trim it with the scissors.

9. Shape the coil so it turns easily with the arms through the loops between both magnets.

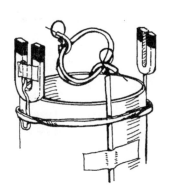

10. Connect the ends of the two long wires opposite the wire loops to the battery, taping one wire to each pole. Blow on the coil to start the motor spinning. If it doesn't start up, blow in the opposite direction.

What makes the motor spin? How is an electromagnet involved? Can you think of other ways to make a motor work?

Now that you have made a motor, think about ways to use a motor like this to do work. Can you make a toy that uses a motor? (*Hint:* In some machines, a shaft from the motor is used to turn a wheel.)

Communicating with Electricity

In 1838, Samuel Morse, building on the discoveries of Franklin, Volta, and Faraday, invented a communications device called the telegraph. The **telegraph** uses the principle of positive and negative charges, a battery, and an electromagnet to communicate over long distances, using a language of taps that sound short or long, or light flashes. It should be no surprise that the language Morse developed for communicating with a telegraph is called **Morse code.** The language uses electrical signals represented by combinations of dots and dashes to send information across long distances. The chart shown here will show you how to "speak" in the version of Morse code originally created by Samuel Morse. A dot means a short tap or flash of light. A dash means a long tap or flash.

Morse Code

Alphabet		Numerals	Punctuation
A ●▬	N ▬●	1 ●▬▬●	(.) ●●▬▬●●
B ▬●●●	O ● ●	2 ●●▬●● ●	(,) ●▬●▬
C ●● ●	P ●●●●●	3 ●●●▬●●	(?) ▬●●▬●
D ▬●●	Q ●●▬●	4 ●●●●▬	(:) ▬●▬ ● ●
E ●	R ● ●●	5 ▬▬▬	(;) ●●● ●●
F ●▬●	S ●●●	6 ●●●●●●	(-) ●●●● ●▬●●
G ▬▬●	T ▬	7 ▬▬●●	(!) ▬▬▬●
H ●●●●	U ●●▬	8 ▬●●●●	(') ●▬●● ●▬●
I ●●	V ●●●▬	9 ▬●●▬	(/) ●●▬ ▬●
J ▬●▬●	W ●▬▬	0 ▬▬	(●●●●● ▬●
K ▬●▬	X ●▬●●		) ●●●●● ●● ●●
L ▬▬	Y ●● ●●		(") ●●▬● ▬●
M ▬▬	Z ●●● ●		(") ●●▬● ▬●▬●

MAKE IT: A Telegraph

Materials

hammer
3-inch (7.5-cm) nail
block of wood
yardstick (meterstick)
3-foot (90-cm) piece of bell wire
2 1-foot (30-cm) pieces of bell wire
small light bulb in holder
knife switch (available in hardware
    stores or electronic-supply stores)

9-volt battery
strip of tin (Ask your
    adult helper to cut
    one from a tin can
    with tin snips).
screwdriver
screw
adult helper

Procedure

1. Ask your adult helper to hammer the nail into one end of the block of wood, leaving most of the nail sticking up.

2. Wind the 3-foot (90-cm) piece of wire around the nail 20 to 30 times. Leave at least 1 foot (30 cm) of wire at each end.

3. Connect one end of the wire you just wound to the light bulb in the holder, and the other end to the knife switch.

4. With the first piece of 1-foot (30-cm) wire, connect the bulb to one end of the battery.

5. Use the second piece of 1-foot (30-cm) wire to connect the battery to the switch. You now have a complete circuit.

6. Ask your adult helper to bend the strip of tin into an S form and fasten it with a small screw to the other end of the block of wood. The tin strip should rest just above (but not touch) the nail. Handle the strip carefully so you don't get cut on the sharp edges.

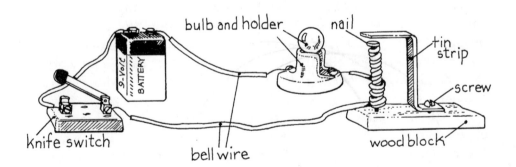

7. To operate your telegraph, tap the switch. Watch the bulb light and the tin strip bend down to the nail head.

When you closed the switch, you completed the circuit. This created a flow of electrons through the wire coils. You produced a magnetic field around the coils, so that the nail became an electromagnet. The electromagnet drew the tin strip down to the nail. The strip springs back up when the circuit is broken, and the magnetic force disappears. The telegraph sends coded messages from the switch to the tin, which makes long and short taps on the nail, and to the light, which flashes.

Now that you have a working model of a telegraph, you need to use it. Try to build two sending/receiving stations attached to each other, so that you can communicate with a friend. To do this, you will need a lot more wire and a second set of materials for a sending station. Try to devise your own uncrackable code, so no one can read your messages.

The Rest of the Story

If you've worked through this chapter, you've made it to the mid-1800s. But that's just the start of the electrical revolution. With the work of people like Nikola Tesla, Alexander Graham Bell, and Thomas Edison, electricity really took off. And after these inventors came many others who found new ways to start the flow of electrons, turn coils of wire in a generator, and produce incredible amounts of electricity.

The books in the "What's Next?" section will help you fill in the rest of the story. You may also want to get more information for yourself. For example, you may wonder how a power station works; how electricity gets from the power station to your home and to your radio or how fuses or circuit breakers protect your home. You may even want to know the difference between electricity and electronics.

If these questions interest you, you can call your local electric power company. Many power companies will give you information about how they work and how they serve the community. You may want to ask your parents about the wiring in your home. Or you may want to take your learning into your own hands by experimenting with wires, switches, batteries, and magnets. Before long, you may be building complicated machines. *Remember,* electricity is powerful, and working with it can be dangerous. *Never* experiment with household wires, and *always* have an adult present when you work with electricity.

What Next?

Benjamin Franklin's Science. I. Bernard Cohen. Cambridge, MA: Harvard University Press, 1990.

The First Book of Electricity. Sam and Beryl Epstein. New York: Franklin Watts Publishing, 1977.

How Did We Find Out About Superconductivity? Isaac Asimov. New York: Walker Press, 1988.

Physics for Kids: 49 Easy Experiments with Electricity and Magnetism. Robert W. Wood. Blue Ridge Summit, PA: TAB Books, 1990.

Safe and Simple Electrical Experiments. Rudolf F. Graf. New York: Dover Publications, 1964.

The Thomas Edison Book of Easy and Incredible Experiments. The Thomas Alva Edison Foundation. New York: John Wiley & Sons, 1988.

Wires and Watts: Understanding and Using Electricity. Irwin Math. New York: Aladdin Books Macmillan Publishing Company, 1981.

The Young Scientist Book of Electricity. Philip Chapman. London, England: Usborne Publishing, 1976.

Chapter 4

Making Music

Benjamin Franklin thought music was "the most pleasing science," and he was the first American to invent a musical instrument.

His glass armonica was based on a common instrument, called musical glasses, found throughout the world. Musical glasses are crystal bowls of water that ring when the player strikes them with xylophone mallets or rubs their rims with damp fingers. The sound created by each bowl depends upon the shape of the bowl and the amount of water in it.

Benjamin Franklin, a fine musician, played the harp, guitar, and violin. In 1761, while Franklin was in London as a representative of the American colonies, he attended a musical glasses concert given by Edmund Delavel. By rubbing damp fingers along the rims of crystal wine glasses that contained different amounts of water, Delavel played slow, beautiful melodies, one note at a time. Although Franklin loved Delavel's music, he thought he knew how to improve Delavel's instrument.

Franklin asked a glassblower, Charles James, to make 37 different-sized crystal bowls with holes in the center. First, Franklin lined the bowls up from the smallest to the largest. Then, he ran an iron rod through the holes, and placed the line of bowls in a pan of water. Finally, he attached a wheel to one end of the iron rod, and with a fan belt, connected the iron rod to a foot pedal.

Pumping on the foot pedal caused the rod of bowls to spin in the pan of water. Franklin then dusted his fingers with chalk to create friction so the crystal bowls would ring more loudly when he touched them. He was ready to play! To make music, Ben held his fingers to the wet edges of the bowls as they turned. His fingers started a vibration in the bowls, creating a musical tone. You can make a musical tone in the same way by wetting a finger and running it around the edge of a wine glass—ask permission first!

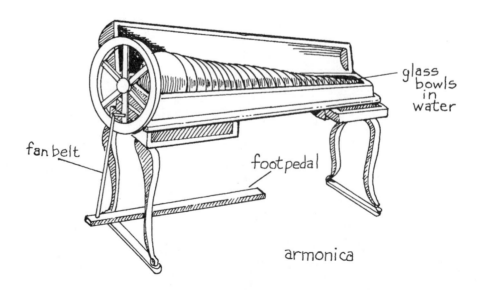

glass bowls in water

fan belt

foot pedal

armonica

With many bowls at his fingertips, Franklin was able to play quick and lively music, in addition to the slow melodies people usually played on musical glasses. The rotating bowls, set in a line like the keys on a piano, also allowed Ben to play many notes at a time, making his music more interesting. That's why Franklin called his new instrument an **armonica,** from the Italian word for "harmony." (The *armonica* is a very different instrument from the *h*armonica, which is played with the mouth.)

Franklin's invention was an instant success. His friends George Washington and Thomas Jefferson agreed that the armonica created some of the most beautiful sounds of the century. Many famous composers, such as Wolfgang Amadeus Mozart and Ludwig van Beethoven, created music just for the armonica. The instrument was introduced in Europe, and even Marie Antoinette, the queen of France, took lessons on it.

But soon, people began to notice that musicians who played the armonica every day sometimes got sick. During Franklin's time, doctors thought that the constant rubbing of sensitive fingertips against glass caused the problem. Today, we know that eighteenth-century crystal often contained lead, a poison that entered a musician's bloodstream through the fingertips.

When doctors began to advise "hands off the armonica," other inventors in Europe developed new instruments, like the celestina, which sounded like Franklin's armonica, but had a keyboard connected to mechanical hammers that struck glass bells.

In 1956, the armonica was played during America's celebration of Franklin's 250th birthday. Today, you can still hear the beautiful sound of Franklin's instrument in concerts and on records. Of course, the music is played on armonicas that have no lead in the glasses!

Ben Franklin liked the sound of the musical glasses, but he saw a way to improve the instrument. Instead of simply telling his friends that the instrument could be better, he built the armonica. When he came up with a better idea *and put the idea into action,* Ben Franklin was an inventor.

Hearing the World

Chirping birds, whooshing wind, clinking ice cubes, roaring airplanes. We are constantly bombarded by sounds. But how do sounds reach our ears?

Sound is a form of energy produced when an object or part of an object **vibrates** (rapidly moves back and forth), causing the air around the object to move back and forth as well.

Because of the noises around us, we are constantly surrounded by invisible vibrations, which, when they strike our ears, cause us to perceive sound (or noise). These vibrations are called **sound waves.**

Sound waves travel through the ear canal and strike the **eardrum**—a stretched membrane inside the ear that receives sound vibrations and looks something like the skin of a drum. When sound waves strike the eardrum, the membrane moves back and forth.

Three tiny bones deep inside the ear—the hammer, anvil, and stirrup—pick up and amplify the vibrations of the eardrum. These bones, the smallest in the body, send the vibrations even further inside the ear—to the inner ear.

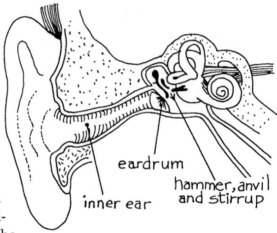

eardrum

inner ear

hammer, anvil and stirrup

The inner ear is filled with fluids that move with the vibrations we hear. These moving fluids cause tiny hairs, called **cilia,** to move. Cilia send electrical messages to the brain—and the brain tells us what we hear! Of course, sound waves are invisible. But to see how a sound wave moves, try this experiment:

DO IT: Make a "Sound Wave"

Materials
clothesline (or any piece of rope)
helper

Procedure

1. Hold one end of the clothesline in one hand, and ask your helper to hold the other end. Stretch the line between you, so that the middle droops almost to the ground.

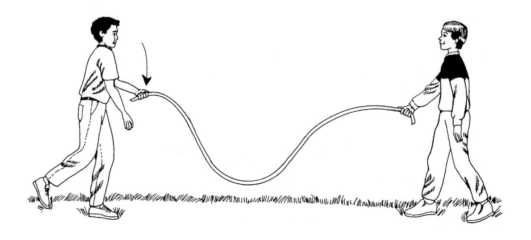

2. While holding your end of the line, raise your hand over your head. Then, snap the line back down. Watch as the line moves up and down toward your friend's end. Now, let your friend snap the line. Try to make the line move up and down quickly. Try to make the line move as slowly as possible.

The up-and-down movement of the clothesline looked like a series of waves. The harder you snapped the line, the faster the waves moved. Like the clothesline, sound waves move up and down through the air. The rate of sound-wave motion, or how fast sound waves move, is called **frequency.** Frequency is measured as the distance between the peaks of each sound wave. Slow rates, or low frequencies, sound low, like the cry of an elephant. Fast rates, or high frequencies, sound high, like a chirping bird.

low frequency

high frequency

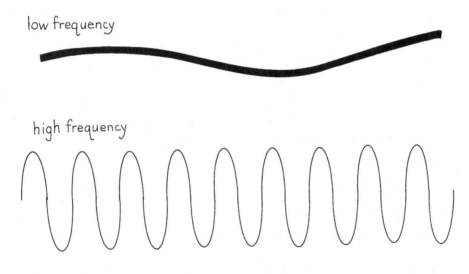

DO IT: Listening to the World Around You

Materials
your ears
timer
pencil
sheet of paper

Procedure

1. Sit down, close your eyes, and try to notice sounds. Remain still for at least 2 minutes, and try to identify each sound you hear.

   If you are outdoors, listen for little sounds, like the wind in the trees, chirping birds, or footsteps. Listen for bigger sounds, too—cars being started, planes flying overhead, sirens wailing, horns honking, people talking. If you are indoors, you might hear a radiator clanking, a clock ticking, a radio or television playing or a baby crying.

2. After about 2 minutes, open your eyes. Now, list all the sounds you heard. How many did you list? If you like, try to notice sounds with a friend, and compare notes. Did she hear something you didn't hear?

3. Organize your list of sounds into categories, or groups of like things. For example, how many musical sounds did you hear? How many engines? How many voices? Did you hear other groups of sounds? What kinds of sounds do you hear the most in your neighborhood?

Creating an Orchestra

Musical instruments create sounds by producing vibrations. The faster the rate of vibration, the higher the frequency of an instrument. **Pitch** is a description of the sound created by an instrument's vibrations. A high frequency creates a high pitch, whereas a low frequency creates a low pitch.

- **Percussion instruments** produce sounds by vibrating materials. Drums, cymbals, and tambourines are percussion instruments.

- **Wind instruments** produce sounds by vibrating columns of air. Clarinets, trumpets, and whistles are wind instruments.

- **String instruments** produce sounds by vibrating one or more strings. Guitars, violins, and harps are string instruments.

With your family and friends, you can create an orchestra. Or, you can pick the instruments you like best and enjoy them on your own. If you decide you enjoy making music, consult the "What's Next?" section for more ideas. And, if you prefer listening to music, you can enjoy many, many different kinds of music on records, cassettes, and CDs and on the radio.

Percussion Instruments

Percussion instruments make noise when two objects strike each other. The objects may be a mallet and a xylophone key, your hand and a drum head, or cymbals.

Here are some percussion instruments you can make. See if you can adjust the frequency (and pitch) of these instruments to make tunes!

MAKE IT: Musical Glasses

Ben Franklin's armonica was based on the musical glasses instrument. You can try out musical glasses in your own kitchen—with your parents' permission.

Materials

pitcher of tap water
several thin glasses (Wine glasses work best.)
helper (optional)

Procedure

1. Pour a little tap water into one glass.

2. Dampen your index finger. Then, gently run your finger around the rim of the glass. Keep going around and around until a ringing sound comes from the glass.

3. Keep running your finger around the rim of the glass. With the other hand (or with the help of another person), add a little more water to the glass. What happens to the sound?

4. Line up the glasses, and pour different amounts of water into each glass. Run your finger around the rim of each glass. Can you make all the glasses play the same note? Can you make them play a scale?

5. Alone or with friends, try to play a tune on the glasses. What would make playing a tune easier? Can you see why Ben Franklin wanted to improve this musical instrument?

When you tapped the glasses, you probably noticed that a glass containing a lot of water produced a lower sound (or pitch) than a glass containing very little water. This difference results because the glass containing a lot of water caused vibrations at a lower frequency than the glass containing very little water.

MAKE IT: Glass Chimes

Here is another version of the musical glasses that uses a spoon for a mallet:

Materials

4 to 8 glasses (Wine glasses work best.)
pitcher of tap water
metal spoon

Procedure

1. Line up the glasses. (If the glasses are identical, that is fine. If they are different, playing a scale becomes challenging.)

2. Pour ¼ cup of tap water into the first glass. Then, pour a little more water into the second glass, even more into the third, and so on.

3. Tap each glass lightly with the rounded side of the metal spoon. Listen carefully to each sound you create.

4. Adjust the amount of water in your classes to create a musical scale (do re mi fa so la ti do). Now, try to play a simple tune on your glass chimes—"Twinkle Twinkle," for instance.

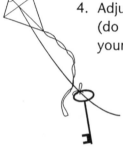

MAKE IT: Maraca

Materials

empty frozen juice can, with both ends removed
piece of cardboard
sharpened pencil
scissors
paper hole-punch
glue
spoon
dried beans (like lentils or black beans) or rice
unsharpened pencil
colored construction paper, glitter, other decorations

Procedure

1. Place one end of the can on the piece of cardboard. With the sharpened pencil trace the can twice to make two circles.

2. Cut out the circles, and punch a hole through the center of each.

3. Glue the first circle to one end of the can, and allow it to dry.

4. Place a spoonful of the dried beans into the can. Hold the can so the beans don't fall out through the hole. Set the can aside.

5. Push the eraser end of the unsharpened pencil through the hole in the second circle. Squeeze glue around the outer edge of the circle.

6. Push the unsharpened pencil into the can until the flat end pokes through the hole at the other end. Press the glued circle into place.

7. After the glue has dried, use the colored construction paper, glitter, foil, or whatever you like to decorate your maraca. To play your maraca, just shake it!

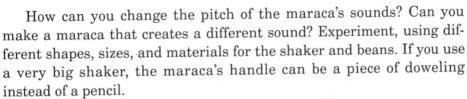

How can you change the pitch of the maraca's sounds? Can you make a maraca that creates a different sound? Experiment, using different shapes, sizes, and materials for the shaker and beans. If you use a very big shaker, the maraca's handle can be a piece of doweling instead of a pencil.

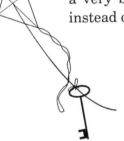

MAKE IT: Drum

Materials
scissors
balloon (in your favorite color)
empty metal coffee can, with one end removed

Procedure

1. Cut the balloon about 1 inch (2.5 cm) from the open end, and discard the small piece.

2. Stretch the balloon over the open end of the can.

3. With your thumbs (or a stick or spoon), tap the balloon drumhead, or pluck it with two fingers.

4. Pull the drumhead more tightly around the can. How does the sound change?

The **pitch** of the sound depended on how fast or how slow the drumhead vibrated. The rate of vibration, or frequency, in turn, depended on the size of the drum and the tension of the drumhead (how tightly it was stretched). The greater the tension on a material (like the balloon), the higher its frequency. A loose drumhead vibrates more slowly than a tight drumhead. So, a loose drumhead has a lower pitch.

Experiment with different types of drum bodies—cups, cans, plastic, wood, and so on. You can even try to make a drum set for your band.

Wind Instruments

Wind instruments use wind—usually a person's breath—to create vibrations. The listener hears these vibrations as sounds. Some wind instruments are the tuba, the whistle, and the flute. You can also think of your voice and your lips as wind instruments.

It's easy to adjust the pitch of most wind instruments. For example, whistle out loud and change the frequency of the sound you make. What changes when you whistle the different notes of a tune?

MAKE IT: Bottle Pipes

Materials
8 identical glass soda bottles
pitcher of tap water
spoon

Procedure

1. Line up the bottles. Pour a small amount of water into the first bottle, a little more into the second bottle, even more into the third bottle, and so on.

2. Blow across the tops of the bottles to create sounds. This may take some practice. Remember—blow *across* the tops of the bottles, and not *into* the bottles.

3. Add or pour out water to adjust the pitch of your bottles. If you like, create a scale (do re mi fa so la ti do).

4. Now, strike the bottles with the spoon. Do you hear the same scale you heard when you blew across the tops of the bottles? What do you think causes any differences you hear?

The bottle pipes created sounds because the air inside the bottles vibrated when you blew across the tops. The more air vibrating inside a bottle, the lower the pitch. Therefore, the bottles that contained the least amount of water and the most air produced the lowest pitch.

MAKE IT: Panpipes

Perhaps you have seen images of the Greek god Pan, with his pointed ears, goat legs, and cloven hooves. If you have, you'll know that this god of forests, pastures, flocks, and shepherds is always shown playing his pipes.

Materials

6 or more plastic drinking straws
ruler
scissors
masking tape
modeling clay

Procedure

1. Lay the straws on a table. Keep one straw whole. Cut 1 inch (2.5 cm) from the first straw, 2 inches (5 cm) from the second straw, and so on. Be sure the fifth straw is at least 1 inch (2.5 cm) long.

2. Tape the straws together so they line up at the base.

3. Plug the bottom of each straw with the clay.

4. To play your panpipes, blow across the top of the straws. You may need to practice to get your pipes to play, but you'll get the knack if you remember to blow across and not into the straws.

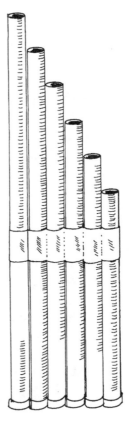

The longer the column of air, the lower the pitch you'll get from the straws. The shorter the air column, the higher the pitch. Can you play a tune with your panpipes? Can you change the pitch on the pipes? How?

MAKE IT: Whistle

Materials
thin plastic drinking straw
scissors
fat plastic drinking straw

Procedure

1. Flatten one end of the thin straw between your teeth. Cut a notch out of one side of the other end of the straw.

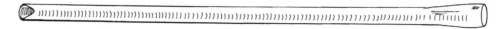

2. Put the cut end of the thin straw into your mouth and blow into it. With a little practice, you'll soon be tooting.

3. Insert the flat end of your new whistle into the fat straw, leaving the cut end of the whistle sticking out.

4. Try whistling as you pull the fat straw to make your whistle longer. What happens to the pitch? Try playing a tune on your whistle "trombone."

Your whistle worked very much like your panpipes. When you blew, you made a column of air vibrate. The longer the column of air, the lower the pitch of the sound you created. Unlike your panpipes, though, the pitch of your whistle is easily adjustable. The fat straw can be extended to make a longer column of air and a lower sound, or it can be shortened to make a shorter column of air and a higher sound. This is how musicians change the notes on a real trombone.

MAKE IT: Kazoo
Here is one of the simplest wind instruments you can make!

Materials
plastic comb
wax paper

Procedure

1. Lay the wax paper on one side of the comb and hold them together at both ends.

2. With your lips slightly open, gently press your mouth on the other side of the comb. Talk through the teeth of the comb. Try humming a song.

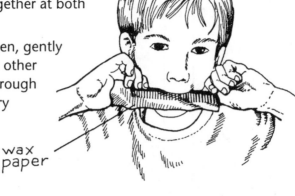

wax paper

By talking or humming through the teeth of the comb, you pushed air toward the wax paper. The vibrations in the air transferred to the paper, which vibrated quickly, creating the kazoo-like sounds you heard. The only way to change the pitch of this instrument is by changing the pitch of your own voice.

String Instruments

It's easy to see a string instrument vibrating—just pluck the strings of a guitar, a banjo, or a violin, and watch them. These vibrating strings create sounds. But if you stretch a rubber band between two fingers and pluck it, you won't hear anything—unless you put your ear next to the vibrating rubber band.

What makes the sounds of string instruments loud enough to hear? The answer is, an **amplifier,** a device to make sounds louder. An amplifier can make a quiet sound much louder. If you've played an electric guitar, you know that you need an electric amp and a speaker to get real sound out of the instrument. But do you know that the hollow body of an acoustic guitar is also an amplifier? And so are the wooden bodies of violins, cellos, banjos, and many other string instruments. The wood vibrates with the strings, creating louder and richer sounds.

Decibels measure the loudness of sounds. The higher the number of decibels, the louder the sound. Some sounds are so loud that people must wear headsets to protect their ears. This "noise thermometer" shows you how many decibels are produced by different sounds.

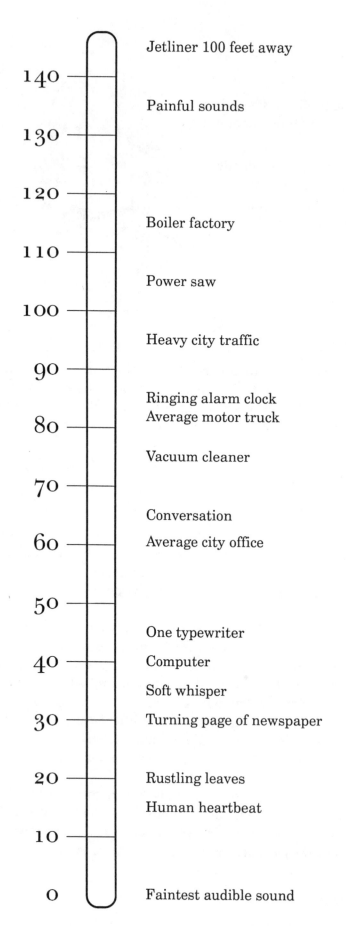

140	Jetliner 100 feet away
130	Painful sounds
120	
110	Boiler factory
100	Power saw
90	Heavy city traffic
80	Ringing alarm clock Average motor truck
70	Vacuum cleaner
60	Conversation Average city office
50	
40	One typewriter Computer
30	Soft whisper Turning page of newspaper
20	Rustling leaves Human heartbeat
10	
0	Faintest audible sound

MAKE IT: Shoe-Box Guitar

Materials

sturdy shoe box, without a lid (or cereal box with the front or back panel removed)

materials for decorating the guitar (glue, glitter, construction paper, marking pens)

at least 4 rubber bands about the same length but of different thicknesses

small, flat board about 3 inches (7.5 cm) wide and slightly longer than the width of the shoe box

Procedure

1. Decorate the shoe box.

2. Wrap the rubber bands around the box the long way, allowing space between the bands.

3. Pluck each rubber band to hear its sound.

4. If you like, insert the board across the top of the box, under the rubber bands. How does the board change the sound of the bands?

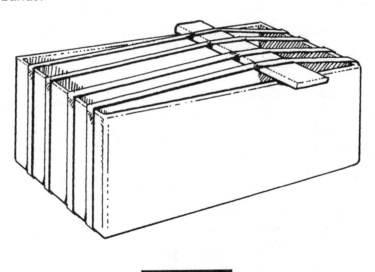

The strips of the guitar vibrated to create sound, and the box **resonated** (vibrated with the vibrations of the strings) to amplify and enhance the sound. You can create different pitches in several ways.

Not only do the length and tension of the strings make a difference, but the thickness of the strings is also important. Experiment with rubber bands of different thicknesses to discover which ones create low and high pitches.

What happens when you pluck a string while holding your finger on the "bridge" made by the board? What happens when you strum your guitar? Try plucking the strings—what happens to the sound?

MAKE IT: Ear Harp

This instrument is a little harder to make than the others, but it is stronger and will last longer. Because the amplifier is only a board, you need to hold this harp up to your ear to hear the rich sounds it creates.

Materials

ruler
pencil
12 × 15-inch (30 × 38-cm) pine board
hammer
6 to 8 small nails
large nail
6 to 8 screw eyes
6 to 8 pieces of nylon fishline
adult helper

Procedure

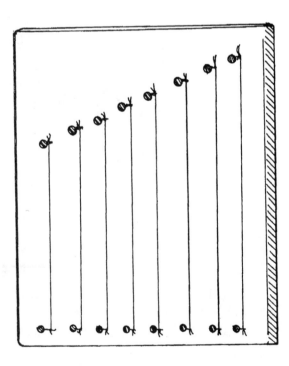

1. Use the ruler to draw a line near and parallel to one of the short edges of the pine board.

2. On the opposite side, draw a line that begins near the edge of the board, and then slants up slightly toward the other side.

3. Ask your adult helper to hammer an evenly spaced row of the small nails partway into the board along the first line you drew. Use as many nails as you plan to have strings for your harp.

4. Using the large nail to start each hole, insert the screw eyes

partway into the board along the other line, opposite the nails. There should be one screw eye above each nail.

5. Tie a piece of fishline between the first nail and the first screw eye, tightening the line before you secure it. Repeat this procedure for the other strings.

6. Tune your harp by turning the screw eyes to tighten or loosen the strings.

━━━━━━

When you tightened the strings, you stretched them, and increased the **tension,** or the tightness of an object after being stretched. When you increase tension, the strings vibrate faster. This creates a sound that is higher pitched.

Making Music

Elements of Music

There is more to making music than just banging on a drum, blowing on a whistle, or strumming on a guitar. Music is a combination of sounds that a musician or composer chooses. A musician's choices may include:

- Pitch

- Melody

- Harmony

- Rhythm

- Timbre

- Form

If you and a group of friends want to make music together, you will have to think about how you want that music to sound. Even if you're playing a simple song, you'll need to make choices.

Pitch

Sound travels in waves. The quicker the rate of wave motion, the higher the frequency of the sound—and the higher the tone, or pitch, you hear.

You already know that it takes work to make your instrument produce the pitch you are looking for. You might want to tighten your drumhead, shorten your panpipes, or adjust the strings on your ear harp to create the pitch you like. Then, experiment with pitch to create a mood or feeling.

Melody

When you play a series of one pitch at a time, you are creating a tune, or **melody.** If you've already tried playing a melody on your instruments, you've probably learned that the glass chimes, ear harp, and whistle lend themselves to melody. Playing a melody on the drum and maracas is more difficult. Try to play "Twinkle Twinkle" on the maraca. Why is it so hard?

Try to play a few melodies on your favorite instruments. Start with something easy, like "Twinkle Twinkle" or "Mary Had a Little Lamb." Then, experiment with your own melodies.

Harmony

When you play several pitches at the same time, you are creating **harmony.** Some harmonies are pleasant to the ears, and others are harsh. Everyone has a different idea about the kinds of sounds that are pleasant—for instance, you and your parents may have different ideas about pleasant and harsh harmonies. And, if you listen to music from different cultures, you will hear harmonies that may sound strange to you.

On some of the instruments you have created—especially the shoebox guitar and ear harp—you will find it easy to play several pitches at the same time. But you can also do this on your glass chimes, musical glasses, and other instruments. Play around with harmonies to find out what sounds please you the most.

Rhythm

A **rhythm** is a pattern of beats, which can be simple or complex. Although you can create a rhythm with any instrument, the most common rhythm instrument is the drum. Other percussion instruments, such as the maraca, the tambourine, and so on, are also important rhythm instruments.

Listen to rock music, and try to imitate the drummer on your own drum. Is it hard to keep up with the drummer? Now, try to create your own rhythms. If you want to use both hands, use two spoons—or beat on a tabletop.

Timbre

Try to play a note on a whistle. Then, play the same note on the glass chimes. The pitch is the same, but why do the two instruments sound different? The answer is that the **timbre**—the quality of a sound as played on a particular musical instrument—is different. Musicians call this difference tone color.

What makes one tone a different "color" from another? When we use a prism (see Chapter 6 on light) to break up white light, we see that white light is made up of many different colors—red, orange, yellow, green, blue, indigo, and violet. In the same way, each pitch actually consists of many pitches that blend. The combination of pitches is different for every instrument.

Form

When all of the above are put into action, we become aware of various melodic, rhythmic, and timbral patterns, usually organized into verses and choruses. Our sense of these patterns is called musical form. There are a variety of musical forms, and they are what is used to create some of your favorite songs.

Discovering Your Taste in Music

What kinds of music do you like best? Rock? Folk? Classical? Many different kinds?

Play your favorite songs a few times, listening to them closely. What kinds of instruments do you hear? Can you pick out the percussion, string, and wind instruments?

Listen for different elements of the music. Do you enjoy music with a fast tempo? Do you prefer complex or simple rhythms? Do you like melodies you can hum? What elements do your favorite songs have in common?

If you are really getting interested in music, visit your library and borrow recordings from many different cultures. As you listen, you'll discover a rich variety of rhythms, tempos, harmonies, and melodies. Some recordings may not even sound like real music to you. But if you like music, you may enjoy new and different sounds.

Working Together

Many musicians play their music solo, while many others perform in bands or orchestras. Some play music that has been written by other composers; others create their own music.

If you enjoy playing music with a group, you can use the instruments you have made to form your own band. You might start by having three people play—a percussionist, a wind instrumentalist, and a string instrumentalist. See what different combinations of sounds you can create with the different instruments. Then, you can add more people, with their instruments, to the group.

If you prefer, try to play a song you all know, or together make your

own music. If you enjoy playing together, you might consider buying real instruments—and holding regular practice sessions.

Whatever you do with your instruments, remember that *everyone* can make music! In fact, it's a good idea to make some music every day. Try singing along with records, whistling as you work, or learning to play an instrument in your school band. The more you make music, the easier it will be—and the more fun you'll have as a musician!

What Next?

Drums, Tomtoms, and Rattles. Primitive Percussion Instruments for Modern Use. Bernard Mason. New York: Dover Publications, 1974.

Horns, Drums, Rattles and Bells. Flutes, Whistles, and Reeds Singing Strings. Larry Kettlekamp. New York: William Morrow and Company, 1964.

Make Mine Music. Tom Walther. New York: Little, Brown and Company, 1981.

Musical Instruments of the World. The Diagram Group. New York: Facts on File, 1978.

Musical Sound: An Introduction to the Physics of Music. Michael J. Moravcsik. New York: Paragon House, 1987.

Physics for Kids: 49 Easy Experiments with Acoustics. Robert W. Wood. Blue Ridge Summit, PA: TAB Books, 1991.

The Science Book of Sound. Neil Ardley. New York: Gulliver Books, Harcourt Brace Jovanovich, 1991.

The Science of Music. Melvin Berger. New York: Thomas Y. Crowell, 1989.

Sound and Music. Neil Ardley. New York: Franklin Watts, 1984.

Wonders of Speech. Alvin and Virginia Silverstein. New York: Morrow Junior Books, 1988.

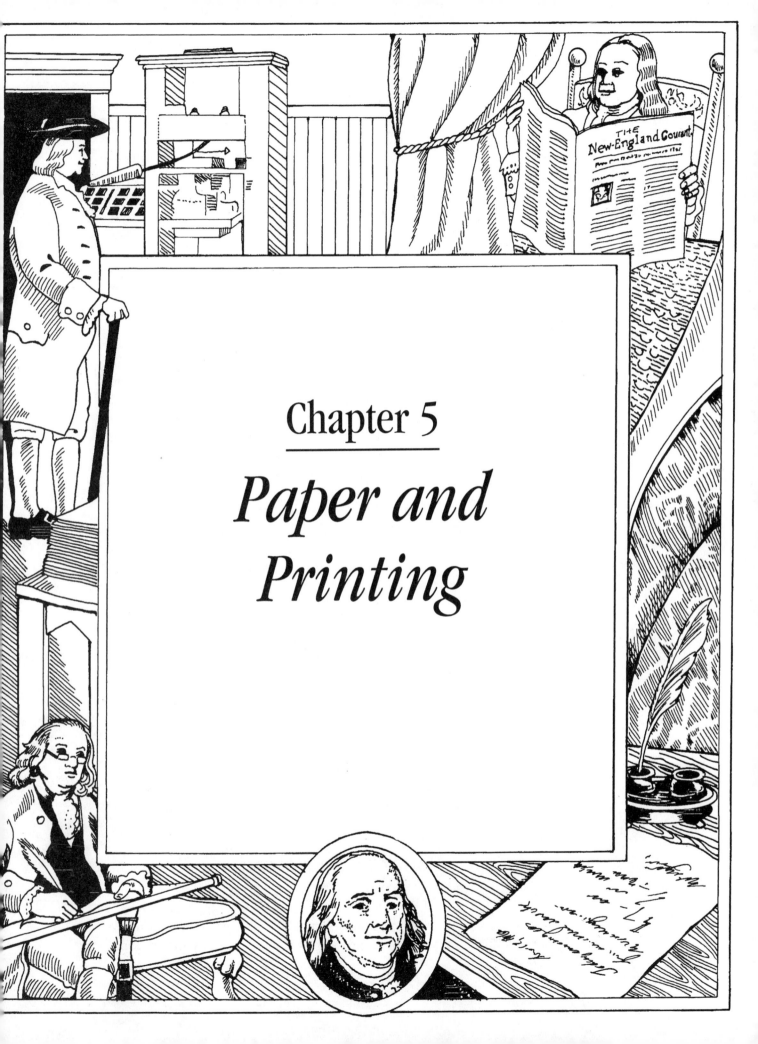

Chapter 5

Paper and Printing

Long before Ben Franklin flew his kite or took part in the American Revolution, he was a printer and publisher. He learned the printing business from his brother, James, who published a Boston newspaper called *The New-England Courant.*

Like many Bostonians before the American Revolution, James felt oppressed by British colonial rule. Unlike most people of his time, however, James chose to publish his ideas. But the British were harsh on people who criticized their policies, and James was jailed for his writings. As a result, at the age of 16, Ben became the temporary publisher of *The New-England Courant.*

Most people assumed that Ben was too young to take the job of publisher seriously. They were wrong. He wrote the entire eighth volume of the newspaper himself, signing it "Dogood." In one article he quoted the *London Journal:* "Without freedom of thought there can be no such thing as wisdom; and no such thing as public liberty without freedom of speech; which is the right of every man . . . ."

When James returned to the paper, he continued to attack British policies. Very quickly, the British banned James from the newspaper business—and Ben became the permanent publisher of *The New-England Courant.*

Ben's apprenticeship to his brother in Boston had taught him something about publishing, but little about the printing process. **Printing** is the art and science of producing multiple copies of words and images on paper. In the mid-1700s, the printing industry in the American colonies was primitive—partly because all paper and printing supplies had to be imported from England.

Ben wanted to know more about the printing business, so he worked for publishers in London, England. At British printing shops run by Samuel Palmer and John Watts, he learned about inks and printing presses. He also learned about new styles of **type** (designs for letters used in printing) and new techniques for **type casting** (making the metal stamps used in printing). By the time he returned to the colonies, Ben knew more about the printing business than most American printers. He was ready to set up shop for himself.

By 1743, Ben Franklin owned and ran three printing houses in three different colonies, and was planning a fourth. In addition to his skill as a writer and printer, Ben had discovered his talent as a businessman.

Paper and Printing in the American Colonies

Today, we take papermaking and printing for granted. Paper is made from trees that may be grown expressly for the purpose of papermaking.

Now, printing—including writing copy, typesetting, layout, and even graphic design—is done on computers. Inks are made from synthetic materials that have been processed in factories. There are dozens of printing presses in every large city. Copies of printed material can be run off on photocopying machines. Many publishing companies use recycled paper to help save trees and protect the environment. New soy-based inks are nontoxic, so they don't harm animals or plants.

In Ben Franklin's day, papermaking and printing were difficult, time-consuming, and expensive processes. Paper was made from rags instead of wood, and fabric in the colonies was scarce, and therefore expensive. Most of the tools used in the printing business had to be imported at great expense from England and the European continent.

Because most of the paper used in the American colonies came from England, the English were able to control the spread of new ideas. Publications that opposed the British point of view found themselves unable to buy paper. Limited paper meant few publications; few publications led to limited communication among people in the colonies.

Some of the first American paper mills were located in Pennsylvania. These new mills were important because they allowed Americans to publish their ideas more widely and more frequently. As paper became available, the people in the colonies could exchange ideas easily and freely. In the long run, paper and printing played an important role in the American Revolution. Ben Franklin's presses—and his published words—were significant in that revolution.

Creating a Paper Mill

Ben Franklin did not make his own paper, although he had investments in paper mills. But you can make paper in much the same way colonial papermakers did. You can then use this paper in the "printing house" you will set up in the next set of activities. Remember, though, that colonial papermakers generally used disintegrating rags to make paper. Today, rags are still used to make extra-strong paper. Look at a box of fine writing paper, and you will probably see that the paper was made with 25 percent or 50 percent rag.

MAKE IT: Homemade Paper

Materials

paper (Bathroom tissue or tissue paper works well. But because newspaper has already been recycled, its fibers are too short to make good homemade paper. Any paper with ink on it will produce grayish paper.)

plastic bowl

warm tap water

blender (optional)

6 × 6-inch (15 × 15-cm) piece of window screening (available at hardware stores). Tape over any sharp edges.

baking pan (slightly larger than the screening)

newspaper

rolling pin

Procedure

1. Tear the paper into very small pieces in the bowl. Pour in the warm water. Pull the paper to bits with your fingers, or use a blender to make pulp (the mixture should be lumpier than oatmeal). Your mixture should be watery (about 20 percent paper to 80 percent water).

2. Lay the piece of screening on the bottom of the baking pan. Pour the paper mixture onto the screening. Move the screening around until it is evenly covered with pulp.

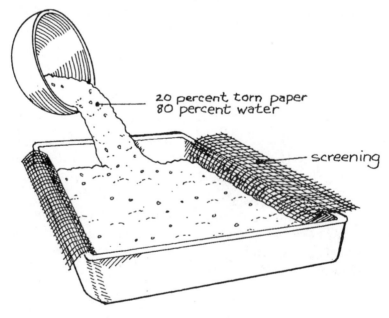

20 percent torn paper
80 percent water

screening

3. Lift the screening out carefully. Hold it level, and let it drain.

4. Place the screening, pulp side up, on newspaper. Place two layers of newspapers on top of the pulp. Use the rolling pin to squeeze the water out of the "sandwich."

two sheets of
newspaper on
top

screening with
pulp side up

newspaper

5. Remove the top layer of newspaper. Turn the sandwich over so that the screening is on top. Remove the newspaper and screening, being careful not to move the pulp. There is your paper! Place newspaper on the pulp and let it dry. Congratulations! You have made a sheet of paper!

Of course, the paper you made doesn't look much like the paper in your notebook or in magazines. But it does look similar to the paper that American papermakers produced during Franklin's lifetime. There are some differences, though.

You can learn to make a real paper mold and nicer paper by following the instructions for the next activity. You will need an adult helper, because this activity requires the use of tools and a trip to the hardware store.

MAKE IT: Mold and Deckle

A **mold and deckle** are the bottom and top of a device used in colonial times to produce paper with square corners and even edges.

Materials

yardstick (meterstick)
board, 8 feet (2 to 3 m) long, 3 inches (7.5 cm) wide, and 1 inch (2.5 cm) deep
pencil
saw
medium sandpaper (optional)
hammer
nails
paintbrush
polyurethane or other waterproof sealant

1 square foot (30 square cm) of window screening
tacks
scissors
4-foot (1- to 2-m) piece of adhesive-foam weather stripping
adult helper

Procedure

1. With your adult helper, purchase any of the materials you don't have at home. They should all be available in a hardware store.

2. Measure eight 1-foot (30-cm) lengths of board. Mark off the lengths with the pencil.

3. Ask your adult helper to saw the eight lengths of board. If the ends are rough, you might want to sand them down.

4. Form a square with four of the lengths of board. The tops and bottoms of the square should be 1 inch (2.5 cm) wide, and the sides should be 3 inches (7.5 cm) high. Make sure the ends of the top and bottom pieces are flush against the side pieces (see diagram). Arrange the other four lengths of board into an identical square.

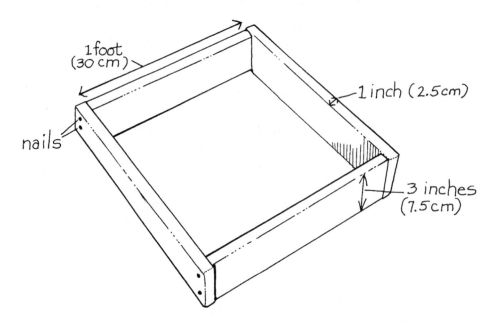

5. Ask your adult helper to nail the first square together, and then to nail the second square together. You should have identical squares.

6. Coat both squares with the waterproof sealant, and let them dry.

7. Lay the window screening on top of the first wooden square. Be careful of sharp edges. With the tacks, secure the screening to the square. Set this square aside.

8. Cut four 1-foot (30-cm) lengths of weather stripping. Pull the adhesive off one of the lengths. Lay it, adhesive side down, along the top of one side of the second wooden square. Stick the other three lengths of weather stripping to the tops of the other three sides of the square. Try to make the lengths flush with one another.

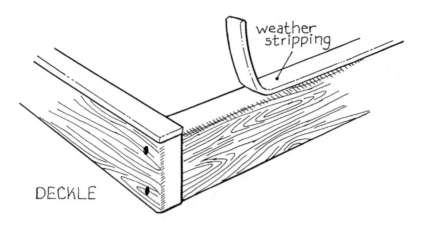

DECKLE

weather stripping

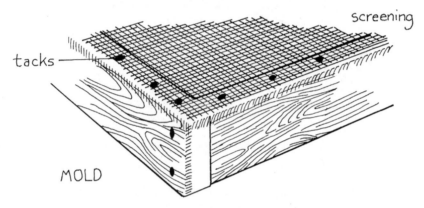

screening

tacks

MOLD

9. Set up the first wooden square so the screening is at the top. Lay the second square on the first square, with the weather stripping side down. The first square is the mold, or bottom. The second square is the deckle, or top.

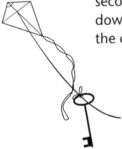

MAKE IT: Using Your Mold and Deckle

Materials

paper pulp (Follow the steps in the
    Homemade Paper activity, page 90.)
plastic bowl
tap water
plastic tub at least 1 foot (30 cm) deep
several heavy books

your mold and deckle
newspaper
several sheets of blotting paper
sponge
sheet of plastic wrap

Procedure

1. Place the paper pulp in the bowl, and set it aside.

2. Pour about 5 inches (12.5 cm) of water into the plastic tub.

3. Set your mold and deckle into the tub, with the mold on the bottom. Be sure the screening is on the top of the mold, and the weather stripping is on the bottom of the deckle. The water should be higher than the screening, but should not cover the deckle.

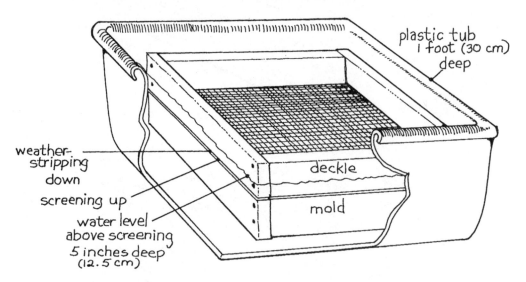

plastic tub
1 foot (30 cm) deep

weather-stripping down

screening up

water level above screening 5 inches deep (12.5 cm)

deckle

mold

4. Pour the pulp into the deckle. Swish your fingers around in the water to spread the pulp evenly.

5. Lift the mold and deckle out of the water, and hold them above the tub to let the extra water drain out. Place the mold and deckle on several layers of newspaper.

6. Slowly and carefully, lift the deckle straight up and off the mold. Your paper will be lying on the screen.

7. To remove the paper from the mold, lay two sheets of the blotting paper on the new sheet of paper. Press down carefully until the water soaks through the blotting paper. Place the sponge on the blotting paper, pressing down to remove more water. Squeeze out the sponge, and keep removing water until there is no more to remove.

sponge

blotting paper

8. Slowly lift the blotting paper off the screen. Your paper should come up with the blotting paper. Lay the blotting paper on a flat surface, with the new sheet of paper on top of it.

9. Using great care, try to peel the new sheet of paper off the blotting paper. If the new paper is not strong enough to be lifted, sandwich it and the blotting paper under it between two more sheets of blotting paper. Use the sponge to press down, so that even more water can be absorbed from the new paper into the blotting paper.

10. When the new paper is strong enough, peel it off the blotting paper. To dry your paper—and to help it maintain its square shape—place it between two more sheets of blotting paper. Place the sheet of plastic wrap on the blotting-paper-and-newspaper sandwich. Place several books on the plastic wrap, and leave it for a day. When you remove the books, you should have a flat, dry, square piece of paper.

Sizing Paper

If you try to write on your paper with a marking pen, you will see that the paper rapidly soaks up the ink. The ink spreads out, making the writing hard to read. This quality is desirable in paper towels, which are designed to absorb liquid, but undesirable in writing paper.

To keep the paper fibers from soaking up ink too rapidly, papermakers use a process called **sizing.** Here are several methods of sizing paper; you can try them all.

MAKE IT: Rubbing (also called burnishing)

Materials
marking pen
your homemade paper
spoon

Procedure

1. Try writing on your paper with the marking pen. Notice that the ink spreads, or "feathers."

2. With the back of the spoon, rub the entire surface of the paper until it looks smooth.

3. Now, write on the paper again. Does the ink spread as much?

The burnishing process smoothed the surface of the paper and forced the surface fibers to fit together more tightly. This process made it harder for the fibers to absorb ink, so the paper was better suited for writing on.

MAKE IT: Gelatin Sizing

In colonial days, people made gelatin from the horns and hooves of horses and cows. They used gelatin to make glue and paper sizing. This method of sizing is very much like the one papermakers used in Franklin's day.

Materials

plain packet of gelatin
saucepan
baking dish
sheet of your homemade paper

timer
dry cloths or paper towels
heavy book
adult helper

Procedure

1. Ask your adult helper to cook the gelatin in the saucepan according to the directions on the packet. When the gelatin is hot, pour it into the baking dish.

2. Let the gelatin sit until it is cool enough to touch—but not so cool that it has gelled.

3. Lay the sheet of your homemade paper in the gelatin. Let it sit for about 2 minutes.

4. Remove the paper from the gelatin, and let it dry on a cloth. When the paper has dried a little, place it on another cloth.

5. Place a heavy book on the cloth-paper-cloth sandwich, and let it sit overnight.

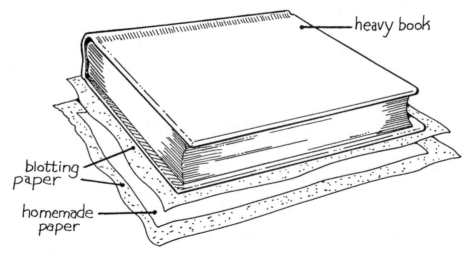

The gelatin coated the paper, so the paper fibers soaked up the ink. This process made your paper better for writing on, because the ink did not feather.

MAKE IT: Starch Sizing

Materials
the materials you used for your homemade paper
tablespoon
cornstarch

Procedure

1. Make paper pulp as in the homemade paper activity on page 90.

2. Before pouring the paper pulp into the baking dish, add a few tablespoons of the cornstarch.

3. Follow the steps for making paper.

━━━━━━━━

The starch filled in the gaps between the paper fibers. If homemade paper is not sized, pools of ink gather between the fibers. Sizing paper with starch keeps the ink from feathering.

Your Own Style of Paper

Now that you know how to make paper, you may want to experiment with papermaking. Start by observing the paper you made. Use a magnifying lens to see that the paper is made up of tiny fibers. Many other items we use every day are made up of fibers—fabrics, for instance—so that rags may be used to make paper. Some vegetables, like pumpkins, have fibrous parts. Corn silk looks and feels a lot like thread. What other objects that you see around you are made of (or with) fibers? Are all of the fibers natural, or are some synthetic? Which ones might be used to make paper?

Think about what you like and don't like about the paper you made. Do you like its color, texture, size, and shape? How can you change your paper to make it the way you want it?

Try changing the papermaking process to make it work well for your purposes. Do you want tough, thick paper to use for construction? Flat, white paper to write on? Beautiful, unusual paper on which to do art work?

You can experiment with any part of the papermaking process. You might change the papermaking recipe, the size or shape of the screen, or the drying process. You can also add steps or ingredients to the process to create new kinds of paper.

Save all the paper you have made—you'll need it for the printing activities that are coming up next!

Creating a Printing House

Instead of making his own paper, Ben Franklin imported paper or bought it in the colonies. But he did his own printing. Some of Franklin's publications are among the best known in American history. *Poor Richard's Almanack,* which Ben wrote and printed, made popular such expressions as, "Early to bed and early to rise, make a man healthy, wealthy and wise." Ben also printed volumes of poetry, pamphlets, magazines, books, and short essays on subjects like the abolition of slavery.

In your printing house, you'll be using some of Ben's methods. You'll also try some processes Franklin may not have used. All of these methods, however, were in use in colonial times.

Letterpress Printing

Letterpress printing is just what the name sounds like: a printing process in which printers press paper down on inked letters made of metal or wood. The printers lined up the letters and clamped them together inside a metal frame to make words. Then, they inked the letters, placed paper on them, and, using a roller (or printing press that used a large screw), created enough pressure to press the inked letters onto the paper.

Typewriters are a form of letterpress printer because they use metal stamps and ink. Compare a sheet of paper on which you have typed a message to a page from a book. What difference do you see?

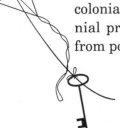

In these activities, you will make letter stamps much like those colonial printers produced. You will also construct a letterpress. Colonial printers, of course, made their tools from metal and wood—not from potatoes and sand!

MAKE IT: Letterpress Stamps

Materials

small, sharp kitchen knife (to be used by your adult helper)
1 small, unpeeled potato for every two stamps you make
marking pen
cutting board
spoon
rulers
tap water
small sponges—one for each color paint you use
tempera or acrylic paints in different colors (available in art-supply stores)
newspaper
your homemade paper (or regular, store-bought paper)
adult helper

Procedure

1. Decide how many stamps you want to make. Do you want to write something special (like your name)? Do you want shapes (like stars and moons)?

2. Ask your adult helper to cut the potatoes in half. With the marking pen, draw the shape you want on the cut side. Remember, your shapes will stick out when they are done, so you need to draw them wide. For example, an A should look like this:

   Also keep in mind that the stamp will print *backwards*. So cut out letters like B and S backwards:

3. On the cutting board, using the knife and spoon, ask your adult helper to carve away the potato around the stamp you drew. Your stamp should stick up about ¼ inch (0.5 cm).

4. When you have cut out enough stamps, dampen the sponges and dip them in the paint.

5. On the newspaper, press your stamp against a sponge. Then, press the stamp against your homemade paper. Follow this procedure for each stamp.

Ben Franklin did not design his own stamps, as you just did. But he brought new typographical designs back from England—and he was the first printer in the American colonies to use those designs. He was also the first printer to import type-casting tools to the colonies.

If you like the way your stamps work, set them aside. If you would like to improve them, experiment with other materials or techniques for making stamps. Remember, the stamps must be hard, they must hold ink, and they must be easy to carve.

MAKE IT: A Letterpress

Once you have made your stamps, you have the main materials for constructing a letterpress. A letterpress allows you to print the same message or image over and over. Letterpresses are used to print many copies of the same message or image.

Materials

more than enough sand to fill a shoe-box cover
2 plastic bowls
tap water
shoe-box cover
small, sharp kitchen knife (to be used by your adult helper)
your stamps
ruler
ice cream stick or spoon
tempera paints (available in art-supply stores)
sponge
sheet of paper (your homemade paper, or regular store-bought paper)
rolling pin
adult helper

Procedure

1. Pour sand into the first bowl. Add water a little at a time, until the sand is damp enough to hold a shape. Be careful not to add so much water that the sand becomes soggy.

2. Fill the shoe-box cover with the damp sand, making sure the sand is level with the edges of the cover.

3. Ask your adult helper to cut the backs off your stamps, so they are about ¾ inch (1 cm) thick.

4. Set the stamps in the order you want them on the sand. Remember, the letters will print backwards, so be careful to set them in the correct order. Then, press the stamps into the sand until the stamp faces are slightly higher than the top of the sand. Use the ice cream stick or the

spoon to help you do this. If you need to, scoop some sand out of the cover to make room for the stamps.

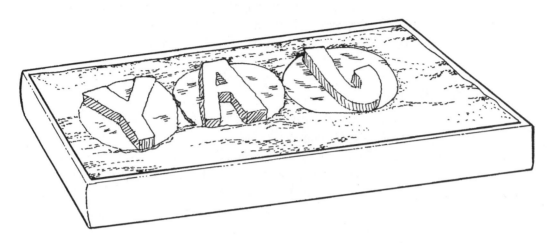

5. Pour some tempera paint into the second bowl, and dip the damp sponge into it. Use the sponge to "ink" your stamps inside the shoe-box cover. If you get some "ink" onto the sand, cover it with a little fresh sand from the first bowl.

6. Place the sheet of paper on the sand and stamps.

7. Run the rolling pin over the paper as if you were rolling out dough. Then, gently lift the paper. Your message (or shape) should be on the paper.

You can use your letterpress to print the same message or shape over and over. So, if you want to make a batch of valentines or birthday cards, your letterpress will come in handy. You can change the message on your letterpress by moving or replacing the stamps. To keep your press from rotting, keep it in the refrigerator!

Engraving

Engraving is another printing process that was used in Ben Franklin's day. **Engraving** is a process in which printers cut designs into metal, then print paper by pressing it into the inked designs. It is almost the opposite of letterpress printing. Instead of making stamps that stick out, engravers cut designs into the metal.

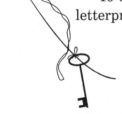

To engrave, you will use many of the same materials you used for letterpress printing.

MAKE IT: Engraving Stamps

Materials
small, sharp kitchen knife (to be used by your adult helper)
several large potatoes or sweet potatoes
pencil with a dull point
ruler
the shoe-box-cover-and-sand press you made in the "A Letterpress" activity on page 100.
fine paintbrush
tempera paint
tap water
soft paper (Paper towels work well.) If you use homemade paper, dampen it before you begin engraving.
rolling pin
spoon (optional)
adult helper

Procedure

1. Ask your adult helper to cut a potato in half lengthwise. You should have a big, flat surface to work with.

2. Use the pencil to cut a design into the half-potato. The design can be words, pictures, or shapes you like.

3. Ask your adult helper to cut

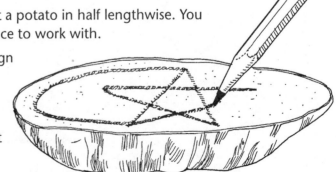

off the back of the potato, so your stamp is only about ¾-inch (1-cm) thick.

4. Remove any old stamps from the shoe-box press, and place the potato in the sand, with the top of the potato level with the top of the press.

5. Use the brush to paint the *inside* of your design with the tempera paint. If you need to, thin the paint with water. Wipe any excess paint off the potato.

6. Place the paper on the press. Then, with the rolling pin, roll the paper as if it were dough. Press down as hard as you can! If you like, use a spoon to press down extra hard on the engraved design. You can even push the paper down into the design.

7. Lift up the paper.

─────────

Like letterpress printing, engraving is used to produce the same image over and over. Engraving is often used for complicated designs, such as book illustrations.

Ben Franklin learned engraving methods in England. He became so good at the technique that, when he returned to the colonies, he was able to print paper money for the state of New Jersey.

Lithography

Lithography is a method of printing based on the fact that oil and water do not mix. To do real lithography, you would need oil-based ink.

This activity is not real lithography, but it uses the same principles as lithography. Instead of using oil-based ink, you will use waxy crayons. Wax, like oil, does not mix with water. So the picture you draw with crayons will not pick up the paint you use as "ink."

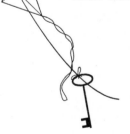

MAKE IT: A Lithography Shop

Materials

crayons
2 sheets of paper
newspaper
paintbrush

watercolors
tap water
rolling pin

Procedure

1. With one crayon, write or draw on the first sheet of paper.

2. Place the paper on the newspaper. With the brush and the watercolors, paint all over the paper. Use lots of water. What happens to the water you paint over the crayon lines?

3. Place the second sheet of paper on the first one. Line up the sheets so the corners match. Use the rolling pin to roll back and forth across the papers.

4. Carefully, peel the second sheet of paper off the first, and then turn it over. There should be watercolor paint everywhere on the paper—except where you drew the design.

5. Lay the second sheet of paper down to dry.

━━━━━━

The wax from the crayon repelled the water from the watercolors. The "ink" was soaked up by the portion of the paper that had no crayon wax on it. When you rolled the second sheet of paper over the inked sheet, the ink from the nonwaxed parts of the first sheet transferred to the second sheet.

Now that you now how to make paper and construct a printing press, you may want to do more in this area. You can use your press to make stationery for yourself or a club. You can use your homemade paper to form beautiful sculptures, or just to write on. Perhaps you'd like to start your own journal on homemade paper. Or you might want to use your new stationery for a club newsletter. Publishing was an important business in Ben's day, and it is just as important today!

What Next?

So far, you have made your own paper in a very simple way. You've also made printing materials that will last only a week or so. If you want to learn more about printing and papermaking, look for some of these books in the library or bookstore:

Paper by Kids. Arnold E. Grummer. Minneapolis, MN: Dillon Press, 1980.
Paper Science Toys. E. Richard Churchill. New York: Sterling Publishing, 1990.
The Papermakers. Leonard Everett Fisher. Boston, MA: David R. Godine, 1986.

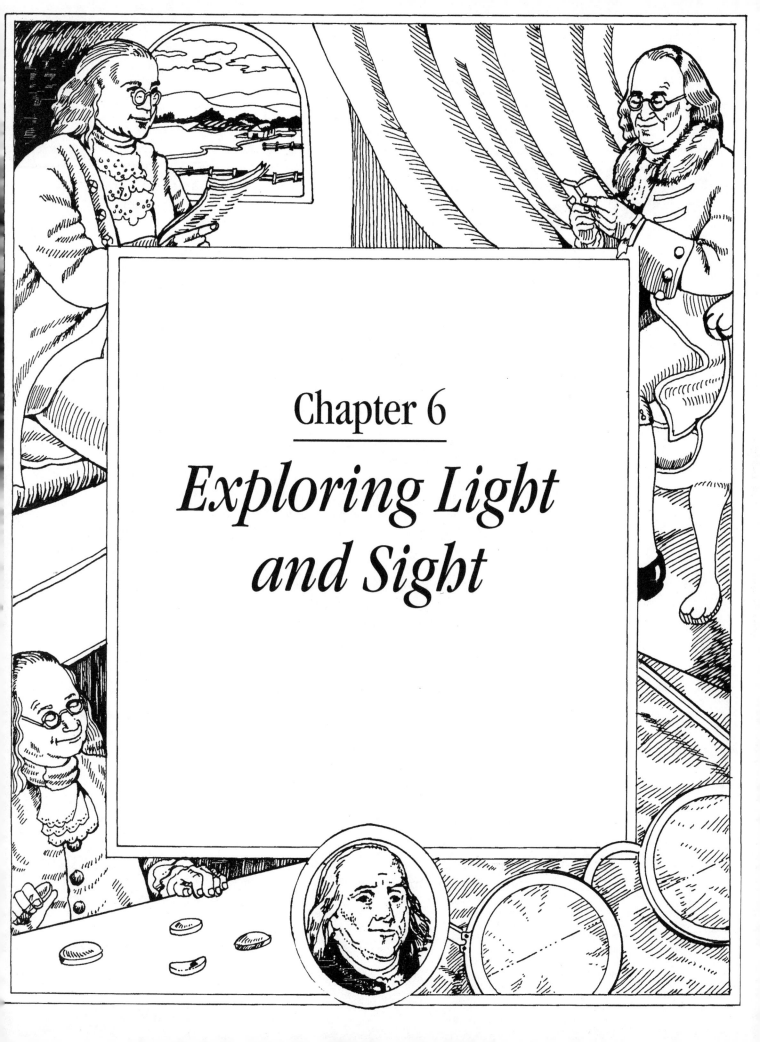

Chapter 6

Exploring Light and Sight

As Ben Franklin got older, he found that he needed two different pairs of eyeglasses—one for reading close up, and one for distance vision. Like many people, he was frustrated by having to change glasses every time he wanted to refocus his eyes. Franklin refused simply to put up with a "necessary inconvenience." Instead, he solved his problem by inventing bifocals. **Bifocals** are eyeglasses with two lenses set into one frame. A **lens** is a piece of clear plastic or glass that is curved to focus light. Usually, the upper lens is used for distance vision, and the lower lens for close-up vision. This is how he described his solution to his friend George Whately:

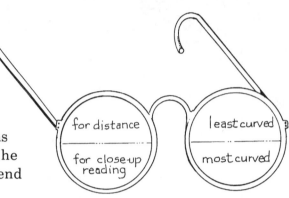

> I had . . . two pair of spectacles which I shifted occasionally as in travelling I sometimes read, and often wanted to regard the prospect [look at the view]. Finding this change troublesome, and not always sufficiently ready, I had the glasses cut, and half of each kind associated in the same circle, thus: By this means, as I wear my spectacles constantly, I have only to move my eyes up or down, as I want to see distinctly far or near, the proper glasses being always ready.

Ben Franklin's invention has made life easier for millions of people for over 200 years. Today, bifocals are often made so you can't see the line between the distance lens and the close-up lens—but the principle is the same.

Franklin was interested in the practical side of lenses and sight. But he also understood *why* differently shaped lenses could help his eyes see objects near or far. To understand the uses of lenses, he had to understand something about the nature of light and sight. In this chapter, you'll see for yourself how lenses work, and discover some interesting properties of light and sight.

MAKE IT: A Lens

Materials
clear plastic wrap
newspaper
tap water

Procedure

1. Lay the plastic wrap on the newspaper.

2. Put a drop of water on the plastic wrap. Notice the shape of the drop of water and what happens to the printing under it.

3. Add more water to the drop, and notice that its shape changes. What is the shape like now? What happens to the printing now that the shape has changed?

Water **refracts,** or changes the direction of a beam of light, in the same way corrective lenses made of plastic or glass do. A water lens is a **convex** lens—that is, it curves *out* in the middle. A lens that curves *in* in the middle is a **concave** lens. To learn a little more about lenses, experiment with convex and concave lenses (available in science-supply stores and some toy stores). What happens to the light when it passes through each kind of lens? What can a concave lens be used for?

Both of the lenses in Ben Franklin's bifocals were convex, but one was helpful for reading close up, and one aided distance vision. Based on your experiment with the water lens, which of Ben's lenses do you think was more convex (curved more in the middle)? Which was less convex? Why?

Nearsightedness occurs when the eye is too long from front to back. Concave lenses are used to reduce the power of the eye so that it can focus far-away objects. Farsightedness occurs when the eye is too short from front to back. Convex lenses are used to increase the eye's focusing power.

Discovering Light

Step into a sunny room, or take a walk outside on a sunny day. Look around you, and notice how light interacts with objects. Does every object seem as bright as every other object, or do some objects seem brighter than others? Are there areas where there is no sunlight at all? Do some materials let light pass through them? What happens to light when it passes through materials other than air? What color is light? Does light make color?

By the time Ben Franklin had invented his bifocals, many scientists had already made the kinds of observations you just made, and had constructed theories to explain the behavior of light. Through experiments, they were able to determine whether their ideas were correct or incorrect. You can carry out your own investigations to help you answer some questions about light.

Before you begin each experiment, write down what you think the answer is to each question. Your theory should be based on observations—that is, on what you see around you. When you have finished your experiment, double-check: Was your theory correct? Why or why not? By conducting a series of experiments like those that follow, you are acting very much like a real scientist.

How Light Travels

Does light travel in a straight line, or does it curve? Can it bounce? Can it be stopped? Before experimenting, write down your answers to these questions, based on careful observation of light around you. Then, go ahead and investigate.

DO IT: Discover How Light Travels

Materials
flashlight
2 mirrors
clear plastic drinking glass
pitcher of tap water
dark-colored construction paper

Spend a little time with these materials, carrying out your own investigations. For example, try shining the flashlight through the pitcher of water, or bouncing the flashlight beam on one or both mirrors. What did you discover about light?

By conducting your own light experiments, you may have discovered rules of the road for light travel:

1. Light travels in a straight line.
2. When light travels from one kind of matter to another kind of matter (for example, from air to water), it bends. You know now that

this bending is called refraction, and you saw refraction in the water lens you made.

3. Light bounces off certain objects. This bouncing is called **reflection.**

Now that you know a little more about light, can you make light bend? Can you stop the path of light? Can you change the path of light? Try the activities below to help you in your light explorations.

DO IT: The Bouncing Light

Materials
flashlight
mirror
clear plastic drinking glass
sheet of black paper or piece of black cloth

Procedure
Shine the flashlight on the mirror, then on the glass, and then on the black paper or cloth. What happens to the light in each case?

DO IT: Where Does Light Go?

Materials
dark-colored construction paper
masking tape

Procedure

1. Make a tube out of the construction paper, securing it with the masking tape.

2. Look through the tube. Can you see anything?

3. Bend the tube a little, and again look through it. Can you see anything?

DO IT: Bending Light

Materials
clear plastic glass filled with tap water
flashlight
masking tape

Procedure

1. Place the glass of water on a table in front of a wall.
2. Shine the flashlight beam on the wall.
3. Mark where the light beam is on the wall with a small piece of tape.
4. Push the glass of water into the light beam.
5. Mark where the light beam is on the wall. What happened?

What Color Is Light?

In the seventeenth century, the famous English scientist Sir Isaac Newton conducted an experiment with light. He passed light through a **prism** (a three-sided glass tube) and noted what he saw. You can repeat Newton's experiment and make the same discoveries he did.

MAKE IT: A Prism

Materials
transparent tape
3 microscope slides (available in
    science-supply stores) or 3 strips
    of clear plastic from a product
    wrapping or other source
modeling clay
tap water

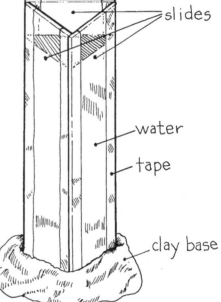

slides
water
tape
clay base

Procedure

1. Tape the three microscope slides together to form a triangle.
2. Press one open end of the triangle into the clay.
3. Fill the triangle with water. You have made a prism!
4. Hold your prism so a bright light, like sunlight or a flashlight, shines onto a dark wall. What happens to the light?

Newton found that light rays hitting a prism break up into many colors. The colors always appear in the same order—and look very much like a rainbow. He and other scientists theorized that light travels in waves—that is, rays of light vibrate at speeds too fast to be seen by the human eye. But all the light in a ray doesn't vibrate at the same speed: the bluer parts of the light vibrate faster than the red parts of the light. When the light ray hits the glass, the light slows down and bends, or refracts. Each color that makes up white light bends a different amount than the other colors. Violet light bends the most, and red light bends the least. Each color exits the prism at a slightly different point; so, we see a band of colors instead of a single beam of light.

The colors you see when you shine light through a prism are called the optical light **spectrum** (red, orange, yellow, green, blue, indigo, and violet). Did you see a rainbow? Another good way to see what happens when white light is broken up into its parts is to blow a bubble on a sunny day.

Newton did not know it, but there is more to the light spectrum than meets the eye. That is, light can do more than simply make objects visible to your eye. Turn on a light, and observe the effect the light has on the area around it. Does it do more than glow? (*Hint: carefully* try feeling the light bulb!)

DO IT: Disappearing Colors

Materials
several sheets of construction paper in a variety of bright colors
You must have access to a room with a light on a dimmer switch.

Procedure

1. Lay the sheets of construction paper in a row. With the light on, note the colors you see.

2. Dim the light. As the light dims, note the colors you see, and how they change. When the light is so dim that you can barely see the paper, note the colors you see.

DO IT: Now You See It, Now You Don't

Materials
5 or 6 pieces of brightly colored clothing
paper bag
large square piece of red cellophane
helper

Procedure

1. Ask your helper secretly to pick out colored pieces of clothing you have never seen. Your helper should put these pieces of clothing into the paper bag.

2. Hold the square of cellophane over your eyes, so you can't see around it.

3. Ask your helper to hold up the pieces of clothing one by one. Can you tell the color of each piece? Why or why not? What difference does the cellophane make in seeing colors?

4. If you like, switch places with your helper. Now you can pick out the pieces of clothing, and your partner can try to decide what color he or she is seeing.

When white light shines on a yellow object, for example, a tennis ball, the object reflects mostly yellow light, but it may also reflect a tiny bit of red light. Your red cellophane is a color filter. Filters work by blocking certain wavelengths of light while allowing other wavelengths to pass through. The red filters allow only red light to pass through. Since the yellow light cannot pass through the red filter, the tennis ball appears red. An object that does not reflect any red light appears dark or black because no color passes through the filter.

More Questions About Light

Now that you know a little about light, you may have questions, such as, How do we see light? What is light made of? What can light do? In the rest of this chapter, you'll learn more about light. But there is much more to know. It's up to you to continue your investigations into this fascinating subject.

For some people, it's easier to notice light through the lens of a camera. If you're one of those people, try this!

DO IT: A Light Journal

Materials
camera
scrapbook
writing materials

Procedure
Use the camera to capture light in as many different ways as you can. Don't use a flash, because that will change the light in your photograph. Try photographing a range of different reflections and refractions. Can you find spectra? How about shadows? Put together a light scrapbook—organizing your pictures by categories. Which images please you the most? Why?

Creating an Optical Toy Shop

Light can make a great toy. It bounces, bends, and creates beautiful patterns—all of them free! Here are a few ideas for making toys that allow you to play with light. Once you've made these toys, try to think of ways to make toys using your own materials, such as mirrors, sequins, magnifying lenses, and other reflective or refractive objects.

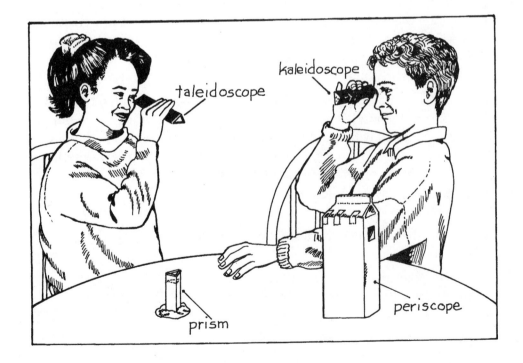

MAKE IT: Taleidoscope/Kaleidoscope

Materials
electrical tape
3 microscope slides (available in science-supply stores) or clear
    plastic from a product wrapping or other source
sheet of transparent plastic wrap
pencil
scissors
transparent tape
confetti, tiny sequins, or tiny beads

Procedure

1. With the electrical tape, join the three microscope slides to form a triangle.

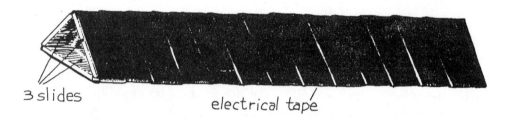

3 slides

electrical tape

2. Wrap the electrical tape around the triangle, so the triangle is completely covered, and only the ends are open.

3. Hold the triangle up to one eye. Slowly, turn it. You have just created
   a taleidoscope! A **taleidoscope** is a three-sided tube with mirrors on
   the inside. When you look through the tube, you see an image
   reflected many times.

4. Now you can go on to make a **kaleidoscope**—a three-sided tube with
   mirrors on the inside and a cap at the end that allows light through.
   The cap is filled with sequins or confetti, and when you look through
   the open end of the tube, you see images of the sequins or confetti
   reflected many times. Place your taleidoscope on the sheet of transparent plastic wrap. Trace around the base of the
   triangle.

5. Cut out the triangle you traced. Repeat to get a
   second triangle.

6. Use the transparent tape to attach the plastic triangles along two sides to make a cone.

7. Place the confetti, sequins, or beads into the
   plastic triangle. Tape the triangle shut.

8. Tape the plastic triangle over one end of your

tape

taleidoscope. Hold the taleidoscope up to the light, and look through it. You have made a kaleidoscope!

A mirror is anything that reflects light rays rather than absorbing them. The glass microscope slides (without the black electrical tape) do not make good mirrors because most of the light passes through the glass rather than reflecting off it. However, when you wrap the black electrical tape around the outside of the triangle formed by the glass microscope slides, the inside of the triangle is able to bounce or reflect the light. The light is reflected over and over in the same pattern, so you see six identical images!

A taleidoscope combines several mirrors to show reflections of reflections. The mirrors can be arranged in many shapes but usually three mirrors form a triangle.

A kaleidoscope is a taleidoscope with an object placed at one end. The object or objects form mirror images that in turn form mirror images of mirror images. The result is a pattern of beautiful, symmetrical images.

MAKE IT: Periscope

See if you can use what you've learned already to create a **periscope**, an optical instrument that lets you look around corners. (*Remember,* mirror images can bounce off each other.) If you like, you can try the following periscope activity:

Materials

empty 1-quart (1-liter) milk or juice carton
scissors
ruler
tape
2 pocket-sized mirrors
adult helper

Procedure

1. Ask your adult helper to carefully open the carton at the top.

2. Then your adult helper should cut a hole in the opposite side near the bottom. Use the ruler to measure that both holes are the same distance from the top and bottom of the carton.

3. Tape the mirrors inside the box, so that they face each other. They should be parallel and slant across the box at a 45-degree angle, as shown in the diagram.

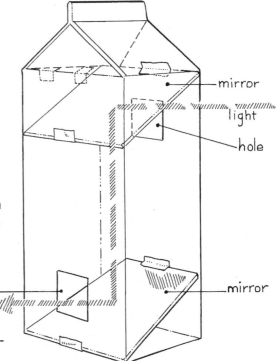

4. After the mirrors have been secured inside the carton, tape the top of the carton closed.

5. Take your periscope to a corner, and hold it so only one hole sticks out. Look through the other hole, and you will be able to see around the corner.

Light always bounces off a mirror at the same angle at which it hits the mirror. If light hits the mirror at a 45-degree angle, it will reflect at 45 degrees, enabling it to make the 90-degree turn around the corner. The light reflecting off the object you look at will bounce off each mirror and into your eye.

How Do You See?

You gather in light with your eyes. But to see—that is, to make sense of the light, shadows, and colors that your eyes show you—you must use your brain.

When light comes into your eye, it is focused by a lens. (The diagram shows the parts of your eye.). A nerve carries the visual information to the brain. When the image reaches the brain, it is upside down, and the brain turns the image right-side up. But even right-side-up globs of light and dark wouldn't mean much to you. You must learn to make sense of those globs.

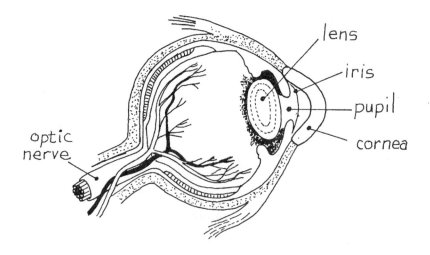

You are not born knowing how to see. In fact, not until babies are several months old do they understand what their eyes are telling them. People who are born blind and then regain their sight have a difficult time making sense out of the information they gather through their eyes. Some people can never make the connection between the

objects they have always felt, heard, tasted, or smelled—and the strange globs of light, shadow, and colors that are now a part of their world. Try this activity to see how our eyes and brains work together to make sense of what we see.

DO IT: Eye and Brain

Materials
pencil
sheet of paper

Procedure

1. Look at each of these images. Then write down what you see.

2. Now, use your imagination. Pretend that you don't know what a circle and a square are, and that you have never seen a puppy. Describe the three figures again. Remember, you can't use the words "circle," "square," or "puppy."

3. Draw a simple picture, or print a word, leaving out part of the picture or word. Ask other people what you have drawn. Experiment to see how much you can leave out of a picture before people can't understand what your picture represents.

Human eyes are constantly sending sight messages to the brain. The brain constantly tries to organize these messages into pictures that make sense. To make a complete picture, your brain will even close or fill in parts of a picture that your eyes don't see—this is called **closure.** Closure seems to have something to do with how you learned to look at things early in life, and it's more likely to happen if the pattern you see is one that is familiar to you. Scientists don't really know how the brain does this.

Even people who have used their eyes all their lives can have trouble making sense of the information their eyes report. Perhaps you have heard of mirages, for example, what look like rippling waves rising from a hot road. These apparent "sights" are actually **optical illusions**—cases of the eye tricking the brain.

Optical illusions can be confusing, but they are also a lot of fun. You have probably seen a few optical illusions in school or in books. In this chapter, you'll learn some visual tricks to fool your friends—and scientific explanations of why these tricks can fool you.

MAKE IT: Birdcage Magic

Materials
pencil
index card
tape

Procedure

1. Trace this birdcage image on the index card.

2. Fold the card in half on the dotted line, with the image on the outside.

3. Tape the folded card to the tip of the pencil.

4. Spin the pencil between your hands as you look at the image. What do you see when you spin the pencil slowly? When you spin the pencil as fast as you can?

When you spin the pencil very fast, your eyes and brain experience persistence of vision. The bird appears to be in the cage, because one message from the eyes to the brain stays for a little while as the next message is coming in. Try to create your own optical illusion based on persistence of vision by using the same tools: index card, pencil, and tape.

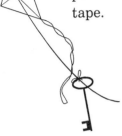

MAKE IT: A Hole in Your Hand

Materials
sheet of construction paper

Procedure

1. Roll the sheet of construction paper into a tube.

2. With your right hand, hold the tube up to your right eye. Put your left hand, palm facing you, next to the tube.

3. Keep both eyes open. What do you see?

You saw a hole in your hand. This optical illusion, called **fusion,** occurs because human beings have two eyes. Each eye sees a slightly different view. The brain fuses, or joins, the two views. You see one image after the eye and brain have done their work. Now that you know the trick, tell your friends that you can make a hole in their hands without hurting them. Then, have each of them hold up the tube next to his or her hand for a surprise!

Can you think of other fun optical illusions you can create using the principle of fusion?

What Next?

Ben Franklin's bifocal lenses were a useful tool. Lenses may be used as tools for many other purposes. For example, lenses allow high magnification when they are used in microscopes or telescopes. They are also used in cameras, powerful spotlights, and planetarium instruments.

Lenses have opened up whole new worlds to scientists—and, in the long run, to everyone who is interested in science and nature. Lenses can lead you out beyond the Earth, to the farthest reaches of the galaxy. And they can help you see the cells and molecules that make up your body.

To make a useful optical tool, you must have high-quality lenses and other equipment. These materials may be expensive. But if you decide you are ready to build a real optical instrument, and you have saved the money to do it, some of the books and organizations listed below can help you get started. If you just want to know more about light, color, and vision, you can continue your experiments—either by coming up with your own ideas, or by getting ideas from these books and organizations:

Fun with Science: Light. Brenda Walpole. New York: Warwick Press, 1987.

Glasses and Contact Lenses: Your Guide to Eyes, Eyewear and Eyecare. Dr. Alvin Silverstein and Virginia Silverstein. Philadelphia: J. B. Lippincott, 1989.

Investigate and Discover Light. Robert Gardner. Englewood Cliffs, NJ: Julian Messner, 1991.

Light Fantastic. Phillip Watson. Lothrop, Lee and Shepard Books, a division of William Morrow, 1982.

Light, Mirrors and Lenses: A Ladybird Junior Science Book. F. E. Newing and R. Bowood. Loughborough, England: Wills and Hapworth, 1962.

Light and Sound. M. L. Alexander. Englewood Cliffs, NJ: Prentice-Hall, 1969.

Light and Vision. Conrad G. Mueller and Mae Rudolph. New York: Time Life Books, 1966.

Mirrors: Finding Out about Properties of Light. Bernie Zubrowski. New York: William Morrow Junior Books, 1992.

More Than Magnifiers. Cary I. Sneider and Alan Gould. Berkeley, CA: Lawrence Hall of Science, University of California, 1988.

The Nature of Light and Color in the Open Air. M. Minnart. New York: Dover Publications, 1954.

Physics for Kids: 49 Easy Experiments with Mechanics. Robert W. Wood. Blue Ridge Summit, PA: TAB Books, 1989.

Glossary

altocumulus clouds fluffy, heaped-up masses of clouds at midlevel of the atmosphere. Alto-cumulus clouds may mean the weather is going to change.

amplifier device to make sounds louder.

anemometer instrument to measure the speed of the wind.

armonica musical instrument invented by Benjamin Franklin. Franklin arranged a series of bowls in a line from the smallest to the largest, ran an iron rod through the holes in the center, and set the line of bowls in a pan of water. He attached a wheel to one end of the iron rod, and with a fan belt, connected the rod to a foot pedal. Pumping on the foot pedal set the rod of bowls spinning in the pan of water. Franklin then dusted his fingers with chalk, to create friction so the crystal bowls would ring loudly when touched.

atomic related to atoms—tiny particles of matter that make up everything we know of in the universe.

barometer instrument to measure changes in air pressure.

battery chemical source of electricity invented by Allessandro Volta.

bifocals eyeglasses with two lenses set into one frame. Usually, the upper lens is used for distance vision and the lower lens for close-up vision.

brainstorming the process of coming up with new ideas, no matter how silly or impractical.

calculations results of using mathematical processes.

calibrate mark with a standard of measurement.

charge when something is charged, it holds electricity.

cilia tiny hairs in the inner ear that send electrical messages to the brain.

circuit electrical connection that uses conductive materials to attach an energy source to an electrical appliance and the appliance back to the energy source.

cirrus clouds feathery wisps, curls, or ringlets, high in the sky. Cirrus clouds often mean fair skies.

clockwise movement in the same direction as the hands of a clock (to the right).

closure make a complete picture. The brain closes or fills in things the eyes don't see.

concave lens a lens that curves *in* in the middle.

conductors materials that carry electricity. Most metals are good conductors.

contract shrink.

convex lens lens that curves *out* in the middle.

counterclockwise movement in the opposite direction as the hands of a clock (to the left).

cumulus clouds puffy and bunched-up clouds at a low level. Cumulus clouds often mean fair weather.

current flow of electric charge.

decibels a measure of the loudness of sounds.

dry cell chemical source of electricity that uses a conductive paste held inside a waterproof case. Dry cells are the batteries used in flashlights and toys.

eardrum membrane inside the ear that receives sound vibrations and looks something like the skin of a drum.

electromagnet magnet that is created by running electricity through coils of wire wrapped around an iron or steel bar.

electrons negatively charged particles that circle the central portions of atoms.

electroscope instrument to detect the presence of electricity.

engraving a process in which engravers cut designs into metal, then print paper by pressing it into the inked designs.

experiment the testing of possible solutions to a problem.

frequency the rate of sound-wave motion, or how fast sound waves move. Frequency is measured as the distance between the peaks of each sound wave. Slow rates, or low frequencies, sound low. like the cry of an elephant. Fast rates, or high frequencies, sound high like the chirping of a bird.

fusion each eye sees a slightly different view. The brain fuses, or joins, the two views. You see one image after the eye and brain have done their work.

generator a machine that produces electric power.

gravity the force of attraction that causes objects to fall to the center of the earth.

harmony the result of playing several pitches at the same time.

humidity a measure of the amount of water vapor in the air.

hygrometer instrument to measure the amount of humidity in the air.

hypothesis an educated guess about the outcome of an experiment.

innovation   the invention of a better way to do or build something that already exists. Franklin developed an innovative stove that worked better than other stoves.

innovator   a person who takes something that already exists and thinks of a new or better way to use it.

invention   an object or process that has never existed before. Franklin invented the lightning rod, which was not known before.

inventor   a person who builds something brand new—something that never existed before.

kaleidoscope   a three-sided tube with mirrors on the inside and a cap at the end that allows light through. The cap is filled with sequins or confetti, and when you look through the open end of the tube, you see images of the sequins or confetti reflected many times.

lens   a piece of clear plastic or glass that is curved to focus light. People wear eyeglasses, made of two lenses, when the natural lenses in their eyes do not focus correctly.

letterpress printing   printing process in which printers press paper down on inked letters made of metal or wood.

lightning rod   a long metal pole that attracts lightning away from houses and leads it into the ground.

lithography   method of printing based on the fact that oil and water do not mix.

magnet   a piece of metal that attracts certain other metals.

melody   the result of playing a series of pitches one at a time.

meteorologists   scientists who study weather.

meteorology   the science of weather.

mold and deckle   the bottom and top of a device used in colonial times to produce paper with square corners and even edges.

Morse code   a language Samuel Morse developed for communicating with a telegraph. The language uses electrical signals represented by combinations of dots and dashes to send information across long distances.

motor   machine that harnesses electricity to do work.

negatively charged   having too many electrons, and therefore holding an electrical charge.

neutral   holding no electrical charge.

nimbus clouds   low, dark-gray clouds, full of water. Nimbus clouds generally mean it is raining or rain is on the way.

nucleus   the central portion of an atom.

optical illusion   the result of the eye tricking the brain into thinking it sees something that isn't really there.

percussion instruments   musical instruments that produce sounds by vibrating materials. Drums, cymbals, and tambourines are percussion instruments.

periscope   optical instrument that allows you to see around corners.

pitch   a description of the sound made by a musical instrument's vibrations. A high pitch is created by a high frequency, and a low pitch is created by a low frequency.

positively charged   having too few electrons, and therefore holding an electrical charge.

pressure   force.

printing   the art and science of producing multiple copies of words and images on paper.

prism   a three-sided piece of glass that breaks up a beam of light into an optical spectrum.

protons   positively charged particles in the central portion of an atom.

reflection   the bouncing of light off certain objects.

refract   change the direction of a beam of light.

relative changes   changes that are compared to earlier changes. Because the weather is always changing, we usually compare the weather to earlier changes—for example saying that we'll be getting cooler, wetter weather than yesterday.

rhythm   pattern of beats. The pattern can be simple or very complex.

repel   push away. A negatively charged object repels a positively charged object.

resonate   vibrate along with the vibrations of a musical instrument to amplify and increase sound.

scientific method   process that includes (1) making a hypothesis, (2) testing the hypothesis through experimentation, (3) analyzing the results of the experiment, and (4) drawing a conclusion based on the analysis. Most scientists use the scientific method.

sizing   process by which paper is treated so the paper fibers won't soak up the ink too rapidly.

sound waves   invisible vibrations, which, when they strike our ears, cause us to perceive sound (or noise).

spectrum   all the wavelengths of light, including those that are invisible (such as ultraviolet and infrared).

static electricity   electricity that is not moving in a circuit. Static electricity may come from lightning, or from a carpet or other charged surfaces.

stratus clouds   calm, flat layers of clouds that spread out at a low level. Stratus clouds may mean an overcast day or approaching rain.

string instruments   musical instruments that produce sounds with one or more vibrating strings. Guitars, violins, and harps are string instruments.

taleidescope   a three-sided tube with mirrors on the inside. When you look through the tube, you see an image reflected many times.

telegraph   machine invented by Samuel Morse. A telegraph uses the principle of positive and negative charges, a battery, and an electromagnet to communicate over long distances using a language of taps that sound short or long, or light flashes.

tension   the tightness of an object after being stretched.

thermometer   instrument to measure temperature—hot and cold.

timbre   the quality of a sound as played on a particular musical instrument.

trends   the direction in which events seem to be moving. In the case of weather, trends may mean fair weather is on the way, or cool weather is leaving.

troubleshooting   problem solving.

type   designs for letters used in printing.

type casting   the process of making the metal stamps used in printing.

vibrate   rapidly move back and forth.

volt   a measure of electrical power named after Alessandro Volta, the inventor of the battery.

wind instruments   musical instruments that produce sounds by a column of vibrating air. Clarinets, trumpets, and whistles are wind instruments.

wind vane   instrument to gauge the direction of the wind.

Index

About the Franklin Institute Science Museum

The Franklin Institute Science Museum, located in downtown Philadelphia, invites visitors to see important scientific and historical artifacts, explore basic science principles with hundreds of hands-on devices, and learn about the technology that is shaping the twenty-first century.

For over 60 years, the Institute has pioneered the development of hands-on science exhibits and has been a leader in promoting broad public understanding of science and technology.

Today, the Franklin Institute Science Museum houses permanent exhibits that trace the history of technology and explain basic science principles in bioscience, communications, transportation, electricity, geology, mathematics, astronomy, and mechanics. The museum also includes a four-story wraparound theater—the Tuttleman Omniverse Theater, the Fels Planetarium, and a working weather station that supplies daily forecasts to area media. It also houses the Greenfield Cutting Edge Gallery, a demonstration area for new products and technology. The Mandell Futures Center galleries showcase technology of the twenty-first century.

The underlying philosophy of the Institute's educational programs is that people learn best by doing. A wide range of learning opportunities—from a walk through an oversized human heart to a search for solar flares using high-powered telescopes in the Institute's rooftop observatory—is offered.

The Franklin Institute also includes the Benjamin Franklin National Memorial, dedicated to Philadelphia's most famous citizen, statesman, inventor, scientist, publisher, and postmaster.